Lags in the Effects of Monetary Policy

A NONPARAMETRIC ANALYSIS

BUSINESS ECONOMICS AND FINANCE

a series of monographs and textbooks

Executive Editor
Arthur B. Laffer
Department of Economics
University of Chicago
Graduate School of Business
Chicago, Illinois

Co-Editor
Gene C. Uselton
Department of Economics
Texas Tech University
College of Arts and Sciences
Lubbock, Texas

Volume 1
Common Globe or Global Commons: Population Regulation and Income Distribution *John C. G. Boot*

Volume 2
Lags in the Effects of Monetary Policy: A Nonparametric Analysis *Gene C. Uselton*

Volumes in Preparation
Demand for Money by Firms *C. R. Coates*

Private Short-Term Capital Flows *Arthur Laffer*

Factor Market Distortions and the Pure Theory of International Trade *Stephen P. Magee*

Demand for Money in Israel *Lewis Mandell*

Other Volumes in Preparation

Lags in the Effects of Monetary Policy

A NONPARAMETRIC ANALYSIS

GENE C. USELTON
Texas Tech University
Lubbock, Texas

MARCEL DEKKER, INC. New York

MARCEL DEKKER, INC.
270 Madison Avenue, New York, New York 10016

LIBRARY OF CONGRESS CATALOG CARD NUMBER: 73-84817
ISBN: 0-8247-6112-x

Current printing (last digit):
10 9 8 7 6 5 4 3 2 1

Printed in the United States of America

Contents

Preface

Numerous attempts to determine the timing and magnitude of the effects of monetary policy have been recorded in the literature. Similar research has dealt with the effects of fiscal policy. Some economists report that the lag between a policy action and its effects is long; others discover short delays. Some studies indicate that the timing of the effects of stabilization policy actions is predictable, others that it is highly irregular. Most of the results have been influenced by the use of statistical techniques designed to do more than identify the timing relationships, e.g., to estimate the elasticity of one time series with respect to another.

The present study uses a well-known nonparametric statistical technique to estimate the timing relationships only—the magnitudes of the effects being irrelevant to the issue. Having determined the length of the period over which the effects of policy are distributed, the researcher is better equipped to use the conventional statistical methods for fitting polynomial functions.

This essay is a revised version of my doctoral thesis, hence the theoretical and institutional aspects of discretionary monetary policy are discussed in some detail. I have resisted the temptation to revise and shorten these sections because of their value to beginning researchers. The manuscript was designed so that an undergraduate student might learn something about the monetary system, "catch-up" quickly on the relevant literature, and begin to do some interesting and important research. If my colleagues in the profession benefit from the introduction of a different approach to time series analysis, so much the better.

Of my debts—which are many—I mention only a few. Professor Stephen L. McDonald carefully read and criticized in detail the entire manuscript. Professor Arthur Laffer read the manuscript and suggested numerous improvements. I am grateful to Professor Stephen P. Magee for many helpful suggestions and for calling a major statistical solecism to my attention. Professors Francis B. May, Clifton Grubbs, Wendell Gordon, and Gerald Higgins all offered constructive criticism. Nevertheless, I claim exclusive responsibility for any remaining deficiencies.

Ms. Mary Dillon and Ms. Jan Stotts labored patiently and efficiently to type several revisions and deserve considerable credit for the quality of the final draft. Ms. Susan Brown provided invaluable research and editorial assistance for which I am grateful.

I am especially grateful to the editors of the *Rocky Mountain Social Sciences Journal* for permission to use some of the materials published in an article in October, 1973.

Gene C. Uselton

Taos, New Mexico
July, 1974

List of Figures

Lags in the Effects of Monetary Policy

A NONPARAMETRIC ANALYSIS

1

Monetary Policy for Economic Stabilization

The Significance of Monetary Lags

This is an attempt to determine the average length and variability of the time period between a given monetary policy decision and the subsequent effect on specific target variables. The nature of the lag in effect of monetary policy is one of the most important issues about which economists have disagreed. It is important because a long or highly variable lag might imply that discretionary stabilization policy is ineffective or, worse, counterproductive.

The Goals of Economic Policy

To put this issue in proper perspective one must understand the economic objectives which have been established by due process. Most elementary textbooks list four goals toward which the nation's economic policies are directed: full employment, price stability, sustainable growth, and equilibrium in the balance of payments. The exogenous variables which the society may manipulate to pursue these goals are usually categorized under the headings "fiscal policy" and "monetary policy."

Fiscal policy has to do with the income and expenditures of government. In periods when unemployment is high due to lack of adequate aggregate demand the federal government[1] may expand its budget and undertake projects involving considerable expenditure of manpower. Such deficit spending is a direct method of intervening in the operation of the economy and temporarily increasing the demand for goods and labor. Similarly, a tax reduction would increase disposable income and thereby permit some expansion of demand. As aggregate demand rises and inventories are depleted, businessmen increase their restocking orders and production is increased. The usual assumption is that output is increased in the short run by increasing the labor input; therefore, employment rises as a result of expansionary fiscal policy. As employment increases so does spending, and the artificially stimulated increase in demand becomes self-sustaining. Theoretically the process can be reversed in a period of inflation caused by excess demand pressure against an economy operating at capacity. A reduction of government expenditures and/or an increase in taxes would reduce aggregate demand, allow inventories to accumulate, reduce the flow of new orders, and cause a decline in total output. As output falls, unemployment rises and the problem of promoting price stability is complicated. It should be noted that the viability of fiscal policy as an economic stabilization tool depends on the condition that government spending is complementary to—not a substitute for—private spending.

Federal fiscal policy is primarily the responsibility of the Congress. The President's budget is prepared by a bureau in the executive department, but the Congress must approve the budget. Furthermore, all spending authorizations must originate as bills in the House of Representatives. The process of formulating a bill in committee, debating it on the House floor and then on the Senate floor, incorporating revisions to overcome various objections of those legislators whose constituents oppose it may involve long periods which could vitiate the effort at stabilization. If there is an additional time lag before fiscal policy actions begin to take effect, then the difficulty is compounded[2].

Monetary policy is a term used to describe those decisions by which the monetary authority exercises some control over the economy. This control operates primarily through actions which are calculated to change the level of reserves of commercial banks. Most monetary theory textbooks list three major "tools" of monetary policy: open market operations, control of reserve requirements, and discount rate determination. These policies are formulated and executed by the Federal Reserve System[3].

The discount rate is the rate of interest which the Federal Reserve banks charge their member banks who borrow in order to make up reserve deficits. Legally, each of the 12 Federal Reserve banks can set the discount rate for its own district (with approval of the Federal Reserve Board); in practice, however, the discount rate is the same in all districts. (In addition to the control associated with the power to change the borrowing costs of commercial banks, the Federal Reserve may exercise a kind of hortatory influence over member-bank borrowing as well.) Discount rate changes are generally viewed as the weakest of the major policy tools of the monetary authority. It may be that a change in the discount rate is most important as an announcement of the intentions of the Federal Reserve.

Open market operations and changes in reserve requirements both affect commercial bank reserves directly; hence they are considered particularly important as stabilization policy tools. Additionally, the fact that the banking system of the United States permits fractional reserves amplifies the importance of the ability of the central bank to determine the level of member bank reserves. Because commercial banks are required to hold only a fraction of their deposit liabilities in reserve, a given change in bank reserves can change the total amount of demand deposits in the system by some multiple of the original change. Theoretically, the expansion factor could be as large as the reciprocal of the reserve requirement, assuming that all banks are completely "loaned up" before and after the change in reserves[4].

The change in excess reserves resulting from a change in the reserve requirement implies a multiple expansion or contraction in total deposits just as open market operations do. This tool, however, is used less frequently by the Federal Reserve than open market operations because even a small change in this variable affects the entire reserve base, and hence would be too powerful in most instances. Reserve requirement adjustments, administered by the Federal Reserve Board, may serve as strong notice to the banking community that a given Federal Reserve policy is to be pursued vigorously.

The Expansion of Bank Credit

Open market operations, the most commonly used of the three major policy tools, are effected by the Federal Open Market Manager, an officer of the Federal Reserve Bank of New York. The Federal Open Market Committee, made up of the seven members of the Federal Reserve Board and five of the 12 Federal Reserve bank presidents, establishes the policy which the Open Market Manager executes. He and his staff, negotiating primarily over the telephone from their offices at the New York Federal Reserve Bank, buy and sell government securities in some systematic way which is intended to accomplish both the long- and short-run objectives outlined in the most recent instructions from the Federal Open Market Committee. Buying securities on the open market, *ceteris paribus,* represents an increase in demand for government securities; thus, their prices tend to rise. As prices rise, the yield on the instruments falls and as a result of arbitrage other interest rates fall. At the same time—and more important perhaps from the standpoint of monetary policy effects—bank reserves rise. The Federal Reserve pays for the securities with checks which are deposited to the securities dealers' accounts in commercial banks. This increase in deposits causes an increase in commercial bank reserves and, therefore, is the basis for a multiple expansion of bank credit. (The reverse, of course, holds for open market sales.) In this way the Open Market Committee can exercise some influence on the level of interest rates and the size of the money stock. Traditionally the monetary authority has been concerned primarily with money market conditions and has regarded yields on government securities as the major indicator for stabilization decisions.

Recently there has been considerable discussion among economists concerning the role of the money stock as a determinant of the level of economic activity. If the level of, say, the gross national product is functionally related to the magnitude of the money stock (or to the rate of change in that magnitude), then control of the supply of money through open market trading in government securities may represent a very powerful instrument for economic stabilization.

The process by which monetary policy may affect such economic aggregates as national income has been rationalized in two different ways. One explanation is that the process is sequential; the Federal Reserve buys securities, bidding up their prices, thus causing their yields and, through arbitrage, other interest rates to fall. The funds with which the securities are purchased become deposits in commercial banks, hence reserves on the basis of which bank credit may be expanded. Falling interest rates induce entrepreneurs to invest in projects which had previously been postponed or rejected and the increased credit availability insures that funds will be available to finance the investments. Increased investment implies increased aggregate demand which stimulates increases in output and employment as explained above.

The second explanation of the adjustment is based on a partial equilibrium approach in which it is assumed that a wealth holder will choose to hold his liquid assets as money and less liquid but interest-bearing alternatives in proportion to the utility yielded by each. The utility derived from holding money proceeds from the various yields related to liquidity. Interest-bearing assets produce future purchasing power. The "representative" individual would be at equilibrium where the marginal rate of substitution of money for the interest-bearing alternative is just equal to the ratio of their respective yields. From the position of equilibrium, an increase in the quantity of money by open market operations would imply a rise in the marginal yields of the interest-bearing substitute (or a decrease in the marginal yield on money). The "representative" individual would observe that his cash holdings relative to his total wealth had increased and, accordingly, would attempt to reestablish the relationship between real balances and wealth (or income) which he had previously selected as appropriate. He would spend at an increased rate until the original ratio of real cash balances to real wealth (or some proxy) had been reached. The increased spending would either cause producers to attempt to increase their output to accommodate the demand or bid up prices (or both). As output rose employment would rise until capacity limitations began to occur, after which the main effect of continued increases to the money stock would be inflation[5]. (Beginning with an "equilibrium" position at less than full employment output is necessary to the argument if changes in the money stock are to influence the level of real output but presents certain logical problems.)

If the second explanation is correct, then the appropriate indicator for monetary policy is clearly the level of the stock of money. On the other hand, if the effect of changes in reserves influences the level of income through changes in investment (and, perhaps, consumption)[6] resulting from changes in the interest rate, then the answer concerning the appropriate indicator is not evident. However, if the elasticity of expectations with respect to price changes of the typical spending unit in an economy is greater than zero, the interest rate may be a poor indicator for monetary policy decisions except in the very short run[7]. For this reason, the level of the money stock may be a more reliable indicator for stabilization purposes. It does not follow, however, that changes in the money stock mirror changes in the policy decisions of the Federal Open Market Committee. Endogenous factors may influence the supply of money so as to reinforce or to counter the policy actions of the monetary authority[8].

Because the fluctuations in the level of the money stock do not reflect exclusively the transactions of the "trading desk," none of the usual measures of the money supply is an adequate proxy for monetary policy. Moreover, "neutralizing" the money stock in such a way as to exclude fluctuations not related to monetary policy actions would not guarantee that the money stock series would be an appropriate indicator of the timing of policy decisions. If the lag between a policy decision and the subsequent effect on the money supply were short and highly regular, then the use of an appropriately adjusted measure of the money stock as a proxy for monetary policy actions could be justified on the grounds that the total lag could be determined by simple addition. There are two reasons for rejecting this assumption: first, there is an absence of empirical evidence to support it. The second objection to the assumption that the time lag between the policy decision and the corresponding change in the stock of money is short and predictable is an a priori argument concerning the process by which changes in reserves affect economic aggregates such as the gross national product (GNP).

The Complete Lag in Effect of Monetary Policy

Open market operations affect commercial bank reserves and short-term interest rates immediately. Ultimately, the Federal Reserve has the power to determine the level of the money stock but this power is by no means quick and sure. The open market trading desk can buy or sell government securities, but resulting changes in the money stock due to the multiple expansion characteristic of a fractional reserve system will reflect the reaction of bankers to changes in reserves as well as preferences of wealthholders concerning their allocation of liquid assets. It seems important to make this rather obvious point because many studies of the lag in effect of monetary policy attempt only to measure the length and variability of the time lag between changes in the money stock and subsequent changes in the level of economic activity. Not only does this approach neglect the time required for the monetary authority to recognize the need for policy action, the time involved in reaching a decision, and the lag between decision and effective implementation, but it systematically excludes the potentially time-consuming process by which changes in reserves induce changes in the level of the money stock. A review of the usual textbook explanation of the money supply expansion process will serve to emphasize the point.

The initial assumption is that all member banks are in the "loaned-up" position; they hold no unwanted excess reserves. The reserve requirement is assumed to be a fraction r of total deposits. Given these conditions and assuming that bankers' liquidity preferences are such that they choose to lend out all additional excess reserves however acquired, a change in reserves ΔR precipitated by open market operations would imply an ultimate change in demand deposits equal to ΔR (1/r), assuming no currency drain[9]. The process by which expansion of this major component of the money stock occurs is crucial.

The holders of government securities (excluding for the moment the central bank, member banks, and the Treasury) are also holders of demand deposits in commercial banks. They pay for purchases of government securities with checks written against their demand accounts and, conversely, payments to them by the Federal Reserve for securities which they sell are deposited in their demand accounts at commercial banks. In either case total reserves change by exactly the amount of the transaction. If the Federal Open Market Committee should instruct the manager at the trading desk to pursue an expansionary policy by purchasing securities on the open market, the first-round effect of a given transaction would be an increase ΔD in commercial bank deposits equal to the price paid for the securities. Under the simplifying assumptions listed above, the banks whose deposit liabilities (reserve assets) had increased would immediately begin to make loans and would continue until their loans outstanding had increased by the factor $1-r$ times the original increase in deposits.

The borrowers, having obtained the funds in order to make major purchases, would write checks to the sellers of those goods. The recipients of the checks would deposit their receipts in their demand accounts and the process of expansion of reserves would begin again, the increment to reserves declining in each succeeding cycle by the factor r times ΔD. After a very few cycles most of the effect on deposits would have been realized. (If the total increase in demand deposits in the illustration is equal to $\Delta D\ (1/r)$, then after only four cycles demand deposits in the system would have increased by

$$\Delta D \sum_{i=1}^{4} (1-r)^i$$

or where r = 0.20, by more than one-half of the sum of the series.)

Unquestionably the average cycle time, the reserve requirement, bankers' liquidity preferences, and a host of other factors will influence the length of the total lag in effect of monetary policy. What is not clear is why there should be any significant time lag between changes in the level of the money stock and related changes in the level of national income. If the process by which the money supply expands and contracts is essentially as described, then at each stage, as new loans are made, expenditures increase by the amount of the loans. These expenditures represent income to those from whom the purchases are made and, if the expansion is to continue, this income must be redeposited in the banking system. Therefore, as the money stock grows, so grows aggregate demand and income. (It is true that many of the purchases for which bank loans are made involve the acquisition of property other than that produced and sold in the current accounting period, but it would be difficult to argue a priori that the percentage of loans for such purchases varies systematically.)

An interesting exception to the argument just presented is the limiting case in which the money stock could expand by precisely the same multiple without increasing credit availability at all. The key to understanding the process by which a multiple expansion of deposits can occur in the absence of credit expansion is an appreciation of the distribution of ownership of the public debt. Of the public debt held by private investors only about 25% is currently held by commercial banks, the balance by mutual savings banks, insurance companies, other corporations, state and local governments, individuals, foreign accounts, and a miscellaneous category including savings and loan associations, nonprofit institutions, corporate pension trust funds, and dealers and brokers[10].

Under strong expansionary instructions from the Open Market Committee the manager of the trading desk may purchase, on balance, a substantial sum of government securities in a relatively short period. If all of the securities which the dealers supply to the Federal Reserve are obtained from investors other than commercial banks, and if the proceeds from these sales are deposited in accounts with commercial banks, then all bankers could conceivably elect to invest the entire increment to unwanted excess reserves in government securities. Because of the stabilization policy being pursued by the Federal Reserve, it must be assumed (in the absence of Treasury funding operations) that the securities being acquired by the commercial banks would be supplied by other private investors. As long as the proceeds from each sale were redeposited in the commercial banking system, the expansion of deposits would continue as usual while the volume of credit remained static. The conditions under which such a sequence of events might occur probably arose in eighteenth-century France[11] and perhaps in the United States in the late 1930s. Certainly under such circumstances the lag in effect of monetary policy would be lengthened. But the increased demand for securities would imply rising securities prices and falling yields on securities (and lower interest rates generally) so that in time the demand for loans of acceptable quality would provide more profitable investment alternatives to bankers. From that point monetary policy should work as hypothesized. Just how long this process would take and whether it would vary greatly are considerations which influence both the length and variability of the lag in effect of monetary policy.

The fact remains that the lag between changes in the money stock and subsequent changes in income is only a part—possibly a minor part—of the total lag in effect of monetary policy. Any meaningful measurement of the monetary policy lag should include the entire period from the time of the policy decision until the effect on the target variable occurs. In fact, some consideration should be given to the possibility that the monetary authority may fail to recognize the need for action the moment it occurs. Fig. 1-1 is an illustration of the relationships of the various components of the total lag.

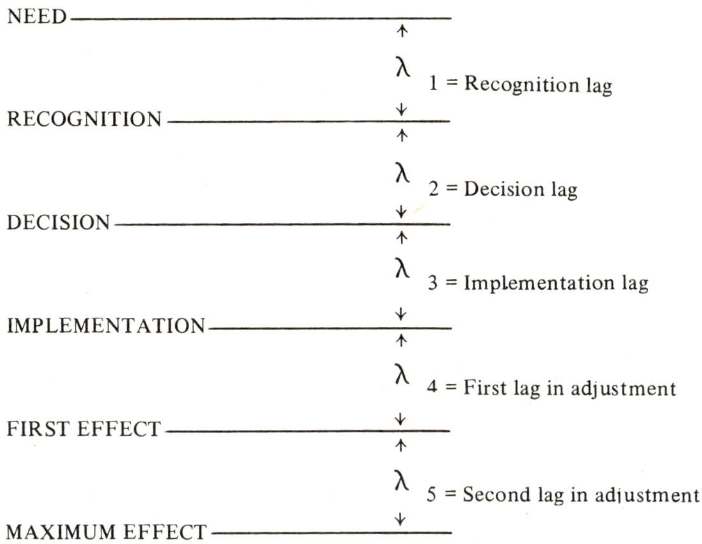

FIG. 1-1 Components of the lag in effect of monetary policy.

The total lag in effect of monetary policy is $L = \Sigma_{i=1}^{5} \lambda_i$, if the time required for recognition of the need for action and the time consumed by the decision-making process are included.

If $\Sigma_{i=1}^{5} \lambda_i > F_r$, where F_r represents the length of a reliable forecast of the target variable, then the possibility exists that a policy aimed at stabilization could have destabilizing effects. Similarly, if $\Sigma\lambda_i$ is highly variable, this could frustrate efforts at stabilization despite a short lag on the average. Note, however, that the recognition lag, λ_i, may be positive, negative, or zero. If for example, λ_1 were negative with absolute magnitude greater than $\Sigma_{i=2}^{5} \lambda_i$, the total lag would be negative; effective stabilization policy could be made on the basis of reliable economic forecasts. The key to the importance of the recognition lag, then, is forecasting. If the time horizon of a reliable economic forecast were longer than the total lag in effect of monetary policy, then only the problem of the unpredictability of the length of the lag would remain to frustrate monetary policy.

It is not within the scope of this book to treat the subject of economic forecasting; therefore, the lag to be measured will include only that period from the making of the policy decision until the maximum effect of that decision on the relevant variable has been realized. Accordingly, while the conclusion that the average lag is very long or highly variable might imply that monetary policy could be destabilizing, proof of a short lag would not be sufficient evidence to validate the argument that monetary policy is in fact a dependable instrument for economic stabilization. Given a short, predictable lag, effective stabilization policy would still depend upon reliable short-run forecasts.

The problem of lags in monetary policy has received considerable attention from professional economists in the past decade; some of the work has been theoretical but much has been empirical. The present study is differentiated from earlier empirical analyses by the use of nonparametric statistics, an approach which provides significant statistical generality in exchange for a negligible loss in power. A review of some of the important parametric analyses will serve as a basis for an explanation of the departure in this study from established methodology. Chapter 2 is a review of selected studies of the lag in effect of monetary policy in the United States.

Notes

1. Government expenditures at all levels affect employment and output, but discretionary countercyclical policy is considered the responsibility of the federal government.

2. Choosing between fiscal and monetary policy for stabilization purposes involves not only the strength of the action and the speed with which it works but also the resource allocation effects. See Thomas Mayer, *Monetary Policy in the United States* (New York: Random House, 1968), pp. 159-165.

3. Some monetary control is exercised by other agencies such as the Treasury Department, but systematic discretionary countercyclical monetary policy is administered only by the Federal Reserve System. See Paul M. Horvitz, *Monetary Policy and the Financial System,* 2d ed. rev. (Englewood Cliffs, N.J.: Prentice-Hall, Inc., 1969), pp. 344-347.

4. The coefficient of expansion of demand deposits is reduced in magnitude by such leakages as increases in the public's holdings of cash and time deposits. Nevertheless, a multiplier effect remains after all of the leakages are deducted.

5. Milton Friedman, "A Theoretical Framework for Monetary Analysis," *Journal of Political Economy,* vol. 78 (March/April 1970), pp. 193-235.

6. James Tobin, "The Interest Elasticity of the Transactions Demand For Cash," *Review of Economics and Statistics,* vol. 38 (August 1956), pp. 241-247.

7. Martin J. Bailey, *National Income and the Price Level* (New York: McGraw-Hill, 1962), pp. 51-54.

8. Patric H. Hendershott, *The Neutralized Money Stock* (Homewood, Ill.: Richard D. Irwin, Inc., 1968), pp. 103-117.

9. Leakages in the system such as allocation of a part of the increase in deposits to currency tend to reduce the magnitude of the multiplier. The value of the coefficient for the United States banking system is at present approximately 2 to 3½. See Mayer, *op. cit.,* p. 84.

10. *Federal Reserve Bulletin,* Vol. 56 (January 1970), A42.

11. See David S. Landes, *The Unbound Prometheus* (Cambridge: Cambridge University Press, 1969), pp. 209-210.

2

Empirical Estimates of the Monetary Lag

The Theoretical Significance of the Lag in Effect of Monetary Policy

The name most commonly associated with the subject of monetary policy lags is that of Professor Milton Friedman. In his presidential address at the Eightieth Annual Meeting of the American Economic Association in December 1967, Professor Friedman made the following criticism of the discretionary monetary policies of the Federal Open Market Committee:

> The reason for the propensity to overreact seems clear: the failure of monetary authorities to allow for the delay between their actions and the subsequent effects on the economy. They tend to determine their actions by today's conditions—but their actions will affect the economy only six or nine or twelve or fifteen months later[1].

The question at issue was the proper role of monetary policy. Friedman argued that the central bank should allow the money supply to grow at a predetermined rate, say, 3 to 5% per year, and abandon its commitment to countercyclical open market operations. His rationale was that the lag between a given change in monetary policy and the corresponding effect on the level of income is both long and highly variable and that, as a result, the efforts at stabilization are likely to be destabilizing. Because of his identification with the issue of monetary policy lags, Professor Friedman's work will be reviewed first.

It will be recognized that arguments advocating a system of rules as opposed to discretionary monetary policy are not new among monetary theorists of the Chicago School. Henry C. Simons presented a persuasive defense of this position in an article published in the *Journal of Political Economy* in 1936[2]. Twelve years later Friedman observed that discretionary fiscal and monetary policy could prove to be ineffective due to problems of timing:

> The lag between the creation of a government deficit and its effects on the behavior of consumers and producers could conceivably be so long and variable that the stimulating effects of the deficit were often operative only after other factors had already brought about a recovery rather than when the initial decline was in progress[3].

The point in mentioning the early objections to discretionary stabilization policy is to emphasize their philosophical origins; even if the lags were short and predictable, discretionary monetary policy could be challenged on other grounds. But the question of the length and variability of the time lags associated with discretionary economic policy is empirical; hence the evidence offered by Friedman in support of his position has been empirical. Even his formal analysis of the problem concerning the timing and magnitude of monetary policy actions, "The Effects of a Full-Employment Policy on Economic Stability: A Formal Analysis," was "suggested by the theory of statistics. . ."[4]. This essay, in which the problem was stated in statistical terms, contains no statistical analysis of data but does provide some useful insights into the lag problem and also into the methodological difficulties involved in devising a solution. The following is a brief summary of the formal analysis in question.

The essay begins by identifying three time series. One represents national income (real or nominal) which would obtain in the absence of full-employment policy. A second series can be regarded as the sequence of additions to or subtractions from the first series resulting from discretionary policy actions. The third is national income including the effects of full-employment policy, that is, the sum of the first two series. Assuming the primary objective of stabilization policy to be the elimination (or dampening) of the amplitude of fluctuations in income, Friedman defined three stationary stochastic series derived from the original series by trend adjustment. If X(t) represents the fluctuations of income in the absence of the effects of stabilization policy, Y(t) the influence of policy action, and Z(t) a trend-adjusted income series, then

$$Z(t) = X(t) + Y(t) \tag{2-1}$$

It is important to note that Y (t) is the combined effects at time t of all countercyclical action whenever taken.

In statistical analysis the variance of a series is a measure of dispersion about the mean, hence an index to the magnitude of fluctuations in the series. The variance of X and Z, respectively, can be regarded as measures of income fluctuations in the absence and in the presence of effects of stabilization policy actions. The variance of Y is an index to the magnitude of the combined effects of policy actions. If X and Y are dependent, then

$$\sigma_Z{}^2 = \sigma_X{}^2 + \sigma_Y{}^2 + 2r_{XY}\sigma_X\sigma_Y \quad [5] \tag{2-2}$$

where r_{XY} is the coefficient of correlation between X and Y; $\sigma_Z{}^2$, $\sigma_X{}^2$, and $\sigma_Y{}^2$ are the variances of Z, X, and Y, respectively; and σ_X and σ_Y are the standard deviations of X and Y. If $\sigma_Y{}^2$ (or σ_Y) is a measure of the magnitude of the effect of countercyclical policy, r_{XY} can be considered a measure of the degree of synchronization of countercyclical policy. If the effects of policy actions were countercyclical, it would be reflected as perfect negative correlation between X and Y; r_{XY} would equal -1. If the effects were completely perverse, hence procyclical, there would be perfect positive correlation between X and Y. If the effect of policy actions were random (in statistical terms, if X and Y were stochastically independent), r_{XY} would equal zero and efforts at stabilization would be counterproductive—not neutral. Friedman's analysis of these possibilities is illuminating; if the ratio of the variance of income including the effects of stabilization policy to the variance of income excluding those effects is less than unity, the policy actions may be said to have increased stability.

If this ratio isgreater than unity, then the effects of policy have been procyclical. If the ratio is exactly unity, the policy actions may be regarded as neutral. Divide Eq. (2-2) through by $\sigma_X{}^2$ to produce the value of the ratio in question.

$$\frac{\sigma_Z{}^2}{\sigma_X{}^2} = 1 + \frac{\sigma_Y{}^2}{\sigma_X{}^2} + 2r_{XY}\frac{\sigma_Y}{\sigma_X} \tag{2-3}$$

From this expression it is clear that effective stabilization policy depends not only on the timing of policy actions but also on the magnitude of their effects:

$$\frac{\sigma_Z{}^2}{\sigma_X{}^2} < 1 \text{ only when } \frac{\sigma_Y{}^2}{\sigma_X{}^2} + 2r_{XY}\frac{\sigma_Y}{\sigma_X} < 0$$

so that a condition necessary for effective stabilization policy is

$$r_{XY} < -\frac{1}{2}\frac{\sigma_Y}{\sigma_X}$$

The policy prescription for complete stability would be to set $\sigma_Y = \sigma_X$. Assuming that the monetary authority could achieve this rather exacting goal, there would still remain the stringent requirement that the timing of their actions be such that r_{XY} would be somewhere in range $-1/2$ to -1. The timing, of course, would depend upon reliable forecasts. The entire essay is a rigorous inquiry into the policy implications of the lag in effect of monetary policy . . . any empirical work by Friedman must be interpreted within the theoretical frame of reference established in "The Effects of a Full-Employment Policy on Economic Stability: A Formal Analysis."

Empirical Analysis of Data for the United States

Friedman alluded to some preliminary results of his empirical inquiries into the lag in effect of monetary policy in a report to the Joint Economic Committee in 1958:

> The evidence suggests that monetary changes take a fairly long time to exert their influence and that the time taken varies considerably. In terms of past experience, for example, action taken now to offset the current recession may affect economic activity in 6 months or not for over a year and 6 months[6].

Detailed explanations of statistical methods are hardly appropriate in such reports. Accordingly, the precise empirical basis for the conclusion was not explained. In the most explicit statement of his recommendations for monetary reform, Friedman did describe some of his early attempts to evaluate discretionary monetary policy:

> Month-by-month, I recorded whether the growth in the seasonally adjusted actual money supply was higher or lower than the growth that would have been produced by a steady 4% rate of growth. I then tried to classify the difference as in the "right" or "wrong" direction according to an objective policy criterion[7].

The purpose of the analysis described was to identify the monetary policy in each period as anticyclical, procyclical, or neutral in reference to general business conditions. As Friedman pointed out, the procedure was highly subjective and arbitrary concerning the selection of variables and lag values. He abandoned this approach to the analysis because: (a) only the direction of change—not the magnitude—was considered, (b) the treatment by individual months implicitly ignored the cumulative effects of the sequence of deviations over time, and (c) discretionary policy would have to be better than the rule substantially more than one-half of the time or it would be destabilizing[8]. These objections are theoretical but it is clear that Friedman did not advance his recommendation for a monetary policy rule on theoretical grounds. On the contrary:

> There are persuasive theoretical grounds for desiring to vary the rate of growth [of the money stock] to offset other factors. The difficulty is that, in practice, we do not know when to do so and by how much. In practice, therefore, deviations from the simple rule have been destabilizing rather than the reverse[9].

Because of the weight of the theoretical argument favoring discretionary stabilization policy—recognized explicitly by Friedman in the preceding quotation—the empirical question concerning the length and variability of the lag in effect of monetary policy has become one of the most crucial considerations in the formulation of any major monetary reform in the United States. Consequently, the selection of input data, the specification of the model, and the statistical techniques employed in empirical studies designed to measure the lag should be subjected to the closest scrutiny.

In his reply to Culbertson's criticism[10] of his empirically based conclusions concerning monetary policy lags, Friedman indicated that his analyses had been of two types: comparisons of "peaks and troughs in the percentage rate of change of the money stock and peaks and troughs in general business as dated by the National Bureau reference chronology"[11], and correlations "between quarter-to-quarter percentage changes in the money stock and the percentage deviations of income and consumption from a trend"[12]. The money stock to which the preceding quotation refers comprises currency in the hands of the public plus all deposits (demand and time) in commercial banks (hereafter designated M_2). The income series is "real per capita income from 1905 to 1951 . . ."[13].

As early as in 1952 Friedman alluded to the fact that empirical work in which he was engaged involved estimating the stock of money as far back as the Civil War[14]. In 1958 he explained in a footnote that the broad findings of his work had been based

> . . . partly on the preliminary results of an extensive study by Anna J. Schwartz and myself under the auspices of the National Bureau of Economic Research on the secular and cyclical behavior of the stock of money in the United States, partly on a series of studies done in the workshop in money and banking at the University of Chicago[15].

Concerning the data submitted in support of their conclusions regarding the relationship between the money stock and business cycles, Friedman and Schwartz wrote:

> The facts we present are drawn largely from our own unpublished work done under the auspices of the National Bureau of Economic Research and associated unpublished work by Philip Cagan[16].

In 1963 Friedman and Schwartz published *A Monetary History of the United States 1867-1960* describing the work in the preface as "a prologue and background for a statistical analysis of the secular and cyclical behavior of money in the United States"[17]. The history is descriptive as well as interpretive, but the details of the construction of the time series and the statistical techniques used in the analysis are largely missing. The authors promised to elaborate on their methodology in a forthcoming work: "Some statistical series we use in this book are explained in full in the forthcoming companion volume, *Trends and Cycles in the Stock of Money in the United States, 1867-1960*"[18]. At this writing, however, the companion volume is not available and it is not feasible to reproduce exactly all of the tests of the time series data which have been performed by Friedman and Schwartz.

But a reasonably detailed explanation of the methodology was provided by Friedman in his celebrated exchange with Culbertson published in the *Journal of Political Economy*.

First, as mentioned above, Friedman compared peaks and troughs in a series representing the percentage rate of change in the M_2 money stock with the reference cycle turning points identified by the National Bureau of Economic Research. (The first series was produced by taking first differences of the natural logarithms of monthly averages in the money stock as defined.) Excluding war years the peaks in the money series were found to precede reference cycle peaks by 16 months on the average. The mean lag between troughs in the percentage rate of change in the money stock and reference cycle troughs was only 12 months. The entire sample included 18 complete cycles between 1870 and 1960 and the peak-to-peak lag varied between a maximum of 29 months to a minimum of 6 months. Given the variables Friedman used and the period analyzed, it is clear that the average lag was long and highly variable.

The percentage rate of change in the money stock series did present some problems. It was highly erratic so that the matter of designating cyclical peaks and troughs necessarily assumed a degree of subjectivity. To obviate this difficulty Friedman devised a system for identifying a "step function consisting of alternating high and low steps"[19]. The "steps" in question were identified by apparent shifts in the level about which the series fluctuated. Friedman described the procedure as "equivalent to approximating the stock-of-money series itself by a series of connected semi-logarithmic straight line segments"[20]. A step peak was defined as that point at which a high step comes to an end, the step trough as the end of a low step. The step dates so determined are approximately the same as the peaks and troughs of the money stock series as it fluctuates about its trend. Friedman pointed out that even these dates preceded peaks in the reference cycle series by about 4 months and troughs by about 5. The implication was that monetary policy actions would have been taken much earlier than these dates. The procedure involving step dates was a means of eliminating some of the subjectivity in the process but the comparison of percentage rates of change with reference cycle dates was more meaningful economically, in Friedman's view. The changes in the rate of change in the money stock were more useful as indicators of the timing of policy actions than maxima and minima in the original series. In either case, the lag was found to be highly unstable so the former was preferred by Friedman on theoretical grounds.

The second technique by which Professor Friedman has estimated the length of the monetary policy lag is correlation and regression analysis. Using quarterly data, he correlated percentage rates of change in the money stock with percentage deviations of income from its trend and found that the highest correlation appeared with the monetary series leading income by three or four quarters. Although the 9- to 12-months lag implied was shorter than the 12- to 16-months average determined by the other method, Friedman believed that the discrepancy was well within the range which could be attributed to sampling error.

Correlation analysis was applied to the two series in a variety of derivative forms. For example, Friedman's work included correlating the stock of money with income, which produced the expected high correlations associated with two series having strong trends in the same direction. In this case the correlations between the two trends were so high that the lag (or lead) relationship did not appear to have much relevance. Another procedure was to fit trends to the two quarterly series by simple graphic methods, then to correlate the percentage deviations of income from its trend with percentage deviations of the stock of money from its trend. This process produced "extremely" low correlations for all reasonable leads or lags, but the correlation coefficient was highest when the series were synchronized. Even the highest correlation, however, was not significantly different from that which could be attributed to pure chance. Friedman attributed the low correlations to the difficulty of fitting a "single satisfactory trend to the money stock"[21].

As a third alternative, first differences of the two series were correlated producing the perplexing result of negative correlation for all leads and lags[22]. When the period in question was limited to 1948 through 1958, the correlation became positive with the highest value appearing when quarter-to-quarter changes in money led similar changes in income by two quarters. Although the result described was not regarded by Friedman as inconsistent with the timing relationship identified by the step date procedure, the correlation coefficient was too low to be statistically important.

In summary, Friedman apparently regarded his correlation analysis of logarithmic first differences of the quarterly M_2 money stock series with percentage deviations of real income from its trend as most significant in the correlation-regression analysis category. Similarly, as indicated before, he preferred the comparison of percentage rates of change in the monthly M_2 money stock series with reference cycle turning points as identified by the National Bureau of Economic Research. The former produced lag values of 9 to 12 months while the latter implied 12 to 16 month lags with money leading income in both cases. Friedman's theoretical argument for choosing these two methods was based on the assumption that changes in the rate of change in the money stock are good indicators of the timing of policy actions of the Federal Reserve. He has left no doubt of the strength of his convictions but he has moderated his policy recommendations in view of the tentative nature of his conclusions:

> . . . the attempt to do more than we can will itself be a disturbance that may increase rather than reduce instability. But like all such injunctions, this one too must be taken in moderation. It is a plea for a sense of perspective and balance, not for irresponsibility in the face of major problems or the failure to correct past mistakes [23].

In addition to the work of Friedman and Schwartz there have been a number of empirical studies dealing with or pertaining to the issue of lags in monetary policy. Some of these studies deal specifically with the subject at hand, as their titles indicate. Others are based on the results obtained from running time series data through complicated econometric models, hence the conclusions concerning monetary policy lags are only minor parts of the results of these analyses. Although the first two groups are mutually exclusive, not all conceivable classifications of the studies are so distinct. For example, one category might be "The Role of the Money Stock in Business Cycles"; another possibility, "Monetary Policy and Economic Stabilization." The point in explaining these distinctions is that many of the studies, although they include materials relating to the lag in effect of monetary policy, were not primarily designed to deal with that rather specific topic. All subsequent criticism of the selection of data or of the methodology used in these studies, then, necessarily takes into account the fact that the approach may have been quite appropriate for the stated objective yet inadequate for an inquiry into the specific subject of monetary policy lags.

Because this analysis treats only the lag in effect of monetary policy in the United States, the studies mentioned will be divided into two groups: those dealing with the United States system, and those dealing with foreign economies. Only those directly concerned with United States statistical data will be considered in any detail. A further limitation will be to exclude the econometric models from detailed review. The two categories excluded involve about one-half of the studies to be considered: for these, only the methodologies and conclusions will be noted.

A statistical analysis which was published in 1959 by Beryl Sprinkel[24] can appropriately be considered immediately following Friedman's work because the methodology is quite similar. Sprinkel was interested primarily in economic forecasting rather than discretionary monetary policy, but his results are not only relevant to the policy question but also appear to support Friedman's claim that the lag is long and highly variable.

In his study Sprinkel compared changes in the growth rate of the money stock, defined as demand deposits in commercial banks plus currency in the hands of the public, with business cycle peaks and troughs as identified by the National Bureau of Economic Research. All of the money stock data were quarterly and three different techniques were used to identify the series which would represent "changes in the rate of growth." None of the three was the precise equivalent of Friedman's "logarithmic first differences" series, but all constitute measures of the percentage change in the rate of growth of the money stock. The three methods of computation were described as follows:

> (1) Series I computed as the per cent change from preceding month;
> (2) Series II computed as a six-month moving average of the per

> cent change from the preceding month plotted on the sixth month; and (3) Series III computed as the per cent change from year-ago data[25].

It was explained in a footnote that the objective in producing the series in the manner described was to generate a measure which would be sensitive to recent changes in the growth rate of the money stock as well as smooth enough to show definite turning points. Series II appears to have been the best compromise. (Friedman's solution, it will be recalled, was to identify step peaks and step troughs in the percentage growth rate series.) Statistically, there is little difference between Sprinkel's measure and Friedman's; hence the agreement of their conclusions is not surprising. The study indicated that the average lag between the money series and general business was shorter for upturns than for downturns. All three of the money series showed long, variable lags; but series II reflected the least variability. The average lag for recoveries was 8.6 months and, for business declines, 19.9 months. (In the contracting series the lag varied from 20 to 29 months.)

Although Sprinkel's main purpose was to test the hypothesis that the growth rate of the money stock was a reliable predictor of the level of business activity, he did offer some comments relevant to discretionary monetary policy. First, the discrepancy between lag lengths in expansions and contractions was rationalized as reflecting the efforts of the public and nonbank enterprises to economize on cash balances during periods of high and rising interest rates. Second, if autonomous variations in the money supply are to be employed for countercyclical purposes, Sprinkel suggested that the length of the lag between policy action and effect will be even longer due to the reactions of commercial bankers to changes in their reserves. The entire study, then, points to the conclusion that discretionary monetary policy formulated and administered by the Federal Reserve is likely to be ineffective due to the long lags.

Results of an earlier inquiry into the connection between monetary policies of the central bank and business fluctuations were published by Clark Warburton in 1950. He wrote:

> In addition, the Federal Reserve authorities did not adequately appraise the degree of lag between their actions in tightening central

> bank credit and the resulting effects on the operations of commercial banks and the consequent impact on business[26].

The article is not so much an argument for abandoning efforts at stabilization through monetary policy as a warning of the consequences of ignoring the lag effect. Warburton's suggestion for measuring the lag was to study the sequential components in the adjustment process implied by some consolidation of the theoretical arguments of the "monetary" and "fiscal" schools[27]. The data used in the analysis were originally published in 1948 in the *Journal of the American Statistical Association,* so the figures deal only with that 30-year period from 1918 through 1947[28]. Having explained that the sequence of adjustment of general business following changes in bank reserves involves two lags, one being the time required for bankers to respond, the other, for prices and output to react to the change in the quantity of money, Warburton wrote: "Under some circumstances the lag may be of negligible duration; under other circumstances as much as or more than a year"[29].

The total lag, then, could be long and certainly was variable, so that discretionary monetary policy might be destabilizing if improperly timed. The details of Warburton's computation methods and his (sometimes subjective) criteria for assigning dates of peaks and troughs are explained in the two articles cited. For purposes of the present study the lag measurements can be divided into two types on the basis of the general business indicator used. The lags appear to have been relatively short when measured as the period between a peak or trough in the percentage deviation from trend of "effective" reserves and the corresponding peak or trough in business reflected in the level of effective demand. Comparing the same monetary indicator with reference cycle peaks and troughs as identified by the National Bureau of Economic Research produced a longer lag on the average. As with the other studies, lags at troughs were shorter on the average than those at peaks: lags at troughs averaging about two quarters by the "demand" criterion and about three quarters using reference dates. The two lag measurements for peaks were approximately four and five quarters for demand and reference cycle criteria respectively.

A study of monetary lags by Kareken and Solow[30] is not only an empirical inquiry into the lag in effect of monetary policy but also a critique of Friedman's methods and views. Only Kareken and Solow's attempt to identify the length and variability of the lag will be considered, the primary objective being to review the methodology and conclusions from each study. Kareken and Solow began by identifying three lags: the inside lag, an intermediate lag, and the outside lag. The inside lag was described as divisible into the recognition lag (the time period between the occurrence of a need for action and the recognition of the need) and the decision lag (the time required for the Federal Reserve to act once having recognized the need). Of these two, the recognition lag was judged to be more important because of its potential length. The intermediate lag was a time period corresponding to that interval between the Federal Reserve's taking action and the instant at which bankers began to face altered conditions. Concerning the outside lag they wrote: "even after firms and households are confronted with a changed supply of money and credit, there is an inevitable lag before real output can be significantly affected"[31]. The inside lag is discrete, according to Kareken and Solow, but the other two components are distributed lags; that is, the effects of a monetary policy action, once taken, tend to begin gradually, to build up to a peak, then to subside. It was this distributed lag which they sought to measure. Nevertheless, a crude estimate of the inside lag, assumed to be exclusively the recognition lag, was made.

Dating peaks in business activity as the beginning of a need for a switch to easy money and troughs as the appropriate signal for a switch to tight money, Kareken and Solow found, for the postaccord period, that the lag was about 8 months in the first case and 3 months in the second. On the question of the intermediate lag, the conclusion was not so clear. Looking only at gross reserves, the investigators found that the Federal Reserve could control reserves with a lag of about 1 month. But they were not entirely satisfied with that figure as an estimate of a lag component, their reason being that monetary policy probably affects aggregate demand through the interest rate. Judging the first effect of monetary policy on the basis of changes in "the" interest rate implied a much longer time lapse for the intermediate lag.

Some of the most interesting and important work done by Kareken and Solow was their analysis of components of the outside lag by economic sectors. For example, they found that inventory investment responds to changes in the interest rate (and perhaps corresponding changes in credit availability) with a relatively short distributed lag such that 25% of the effect is realized in the first quarter, 40% is accumulated by the end of the second quarter, and about two-thirds of the effect by the end of 1 year. The conclusion concerning the response of fixed capital to interest rate changes is less encouraging. It was found that fixed capital responded to changes in long-term interest rates with a very long lag. However, new orders for fixed capital were more responsive, about one-half of the ultimate effect occurring within one quarter, 75% within the first two quarters, and 90% within the first year. Although residential construction was not included in the statistical analysis, Kareken and Solow did estimate the response lag to be no less than 3½ months.

The statistical technique used by Kareken and Solow was "to estimate an infinite distributed-lag relationship by regressing a dependent variable against the current value of the independent variable and lagged values of the dependent variable"[32]. The time series used were quarterly data with a few exceptions in which monthly figures were used to produce quarterly central differences in the money stock series for regressions with deflated gross national product. The disappointing aspect of the study is that the authors failed to provide any specific estimate of the complete lag in effect of monetary policy or, for that matter, of the outside lag as described above for the whole economy. Furthermore, they failed to make clear just what sort of average lag might be implied by the various sectoral lags estimated. (It could be quite long if many of the authors' reservations are justified.) The reader is left with this very general conclusion:

> Our conclusion is that it works neither so slowly as Friedman thinks, nor as quickly and surely as the Federal Reserve itself seems to believe. . . . Some effect comes reasonably quickly and . . . the effects build up over time so that some substantial stabilizing power results after a lapse of time on the order of six or nine months[33].

A much more systematic use of the sectoral approach to lag estimation is exemplified by Thomas Mayer's article "The Inflexibility of Monetary Policy"[34]. The study identified four lags in effect of monetary policy, the first two corresponding exactly to the recognition and implementation lags defined in Chap. 1. The third lag mentioned by Mayer was the time period required for a policy action to change the availability of credit to the borrower. The fourth lag–the only component of the entire lag which Mayer proposed to measure–was described as "the lag between changes in the availability of credit and changes in GNP"[35]. The scope of the study was specifically limited to an evaluation of the timing of monetary policy actions and of their effects; no consideration was given to the strength of the effects. Furthermore, of the two broad functions of discretionary monetary policy actions, insuring liquidity to the system and economic stabilization, only the latter was considered. Lags were measured both for the time required for monetary restraint to have a significant effect on inflation and for the time required for an easy money policy to promote recovery from a recession. (A number of other limiting assumptions were made concerning the strength of a policy action, what constituted a response, etc.) Mayer was obviously cautious concerning the reliability of data relating to monetary policy effects, yet he recognized many limitations in his survey estimates. His final decision concerning methodology was made in view of "the dangers of time series correlation"[36].

On the assumption that monetary policy affects national income through its influence on investment, Mayer identified eight sectors of the economy which together "accounted for over 70 per cent of the sum of all domestic investment (excluding investment by the federal government) plus consumer credit in the period 1953-55"[37]. The eight sectors were grouped broadly under the headings "fixed investment," "inventory investment," and "consumer credit." Mayer utilized testimony of expert witnesses before Congressional committees, personal interviews with those he considered qualified, Department of Commerce data concerning the monthly rates at which various types of construction proceed once contracts have been let, and other such sources. Accordingly, he was able to combine all of the eight sectors into a weighted lag estimate which was intended to approximate the total lag between the change in credit availability and its effect on national income. Mayer's conclusion was that restrictive credit policy will have one-half its effect on investment within 5 months and three-fourths within 9 months. The estimate of expansionary policy lags was even longer: one-half of the effect within 7 months, three-quarters within 10 months. Add to these estimates, conservative according to Mayer, the time required for the investment multiplier to have its effect on income and a long lag emerges—probably of the order of 17 months.

The results of a recent statistical study of Leonall C. Anderson and Jerry L. Jordan[38] contradict the conclusions of the studies which have identified a long and variable lag in the effect of monetary policy. Measurement of the lag was only one of the objectives of the study which was designed to test three hypotheses: "The response of economic activity to fiscal actions relative to that of monetary action is (I) greater, (II) more predictable, and (III) faster"[39]. Multivariate regression techniques were used to estimate the influence of various independent variables on the dependent variable, nominal gross national product, Y. The two measures of monetary policy were M, the money stock (designated in this study as M_1) and B, the monetary base. Fiscal policy actions were approximated by three series described as "high-employment budget surplus R-E, high-employment expenditures E, and high-employment receipts R"[40]. Apparently, successive regressions were run using values for the independent variables in the same period, then one, two, and three quarters earlier than the values of the dependent variable. The data used were seasonally adjusted quarterly averages for the period from the first quarter of 1952 to the second quarter of 1968. Because of the strong upward trend in all of the series, the values used in the actual regressions were first differences.

Proposition (III), which related to the relative speeds with which monetary and fiscal policy acted, is the aspect of the study which deals specifically with the lag in effect of monetary policy. This lag was measured by plotting the beta coefficients for M and B and observing the point at which they reached a peak. When first differences of the money stock were used for the monetary variable, Anderson and Jordan found (as did Kareken and Solow) that the series are almost congruent in the first quarter. The pattern of coefficients in succeeding periods indicated that most of the effect had been realized by the fourth quarter. The beta coefficients for the money variable defined as the monetary base were quite different. No significant effect could be detected with income and the monetary base in the same quarter or with the monetary base leading income by four quarters. However, the pattern of coefficient values rose steadily to a peak in the second-quarter lag and then declined. Assuming that B is an appropriate indicator of the timing of monetary policy, the coefficients appear to substantiate the argument for a relatively short lag.

Another aspect of the testing of Proposition (III) was the development of an Almon lag structure "by using a fourth degree polynomial and constraining the coefficients for t–4 to zero"[41]. This procedure has the appealing characteristic of excluding the cumulative effects of policy from earlier periods from the coefficient for a specific lag value (under the assumptions implied by the technique). The Almon lag, however, was used by Anderson and Jordan only to determine the appropriate time period over which to measure the effects of stabilization policies; the conclusion: four quarters at a maximum. The existence of "relatively short lags and strong effects attributable to monetary actions"[42] implied by the analysis of Anderson and Jordan contradicts the findings of the earlier studies already cited (with the possible exception of the analysis by Kareken and Solow).

Indirect evidence for a long lag was provided by Philip Cagan and Arthur Gandolfi in May 1969[43]. Their analysis was based on the theoretical argument that changes in the supply of money affect aggregate income through changes in the interest rate. The article did not provide a measure of the entire monetary policy lag, only of that portion between a change in the rate of growth of the money stock M_2 and subsequent changes in the rate of interest for the period 1910-1965. The method of estimation was multivariate regression analysis of the form:

$$\Delta i_t = a + \beta_0 \Delta m_t + \beta_1 \Delta m_{t-1} + \beta_2 \Delta m_{t-2} + \cdots + \beta_n \Delta_{t-n}$$

where i is the interest rate, m_t is the monetary growth rate in period t, a and β are parameters, and Δ is an operator indicating the first differences of the variables[44].

The rate of interest proxy was the "commercial paper rate" and all data were monthly. It should be noted that the regression coefficients were unconstrained except by the usual linear least squares criterion. The same data were used with a fifth-degree polynomial function with little change in the results.

According to the pattern of the beta coefficients[45], the effects of changes in the growth rate of the money stock appeared to exert some influence on changes in the interest rate for at least 39 months. (The coefficients were predominantly significant at the 5% level only through the first 23 months.) The sign of the derivative was negative only for the first 6 months and even the cumulative effect became positive after 18 months. On the basis of the 6-month lag in the peak of the cumulative effect and the subsequent declining influence (and, perhaps later, perverse effect) of the policy variable, Cagan and Gandolfi concluded that the ultimate effect of monetary policy actions on the level of income would occur only after a long lag and that, therefore, the potential effectiveness of discretionary monetary policy was in serious doubt.

Objecting to the inherent biases of single equation models of complex economic phenomena, J. Ernest Tanner developed a two-sector model based on an IS–LM analysis[46]. His "estimation procedure used two-stage least squares in order to take explicit account of the interrelation between the commodity and money markets"[47]. Quarterly data for the period from 1947 to 1967 were used to develop structural parameters for current and lagged values of the independent variables. The study was actually designed to test an hypothesis advanced by Tucker[48] to the effect that a long lag in the effect of monetary policy actions on investment is not inconsistent with relatively short lags in the effect on economic activity in general. The argument for this position was that changes in the quantity of money demanded due to changes in interest rates may occur only with a substantial lag. If so, the investment lag could be counterbalanced by the demand for money lag so that increases, for example, in the money stock may be translated initially into consumption and inventory investment effects while the interest rate falls, at first, beyond the level required to stimulate plant and equipment investment. At very low interest rates investment projects of all types would become more attractive whereas the high prices of interest-bearing assets would stimulate an increased holding of money and close substitutes. Tanner's model was developed to cope with these offsetting lags and to give a time estimate of the actual net distributed lag in effect of monetary policy. His conclusion was that "the bulk of the effects on aggregate demand of monetary policy can occur within three to six months of the change in the money supply"[49]. Assuming that the time horizon of reliable economic forecasts is longer than 6 months, Tanner's work is evidence on the side of those who claim that discretionary monetary policy can be used effectively for economic stabilization.

Complementing the studies of the outside lag is an empirical analysis of an intermediate lag reported by William R. Bryan in a communication to the *American Economic Review*[50]. The study is complementary in two ways: first, it provides empirical evidence concerning the length of the intermediate lag; and second, it illustrates the effects of data aggregation and time-period consolidation. Bryan's technique was to use linear regression analysis on weekly data for an 8-year period (1957-1964). The data were collected from 19 individual banks in the Eighth Federal Reserve District and the first lag estimates were made on a microeconomic level. These regressions led to the conclusion that the average time required for banks to respond to a change in central bank monetary policy was approximately 3.2 weeks. The same data were then aggregated and the lag estimate rose to 5.2 weeks. Finally, the original data were transformed to aggregate monthly averages and the estimate of the intermediate lag became

28.7 months. Bryan concluded that parameter estimates based on aggregated data may be of little value in estimating the bankers' response lag and that macroeconomic estimates using quarterly data are apt to be biased toward long lags.

Analysis of Foreign Data

The studies which have been discussed to this point are all empirical analyses of United States data. Several studies of the lag in effect of monetary policy have been made using foreign data; and although the present work involves only the domestic aspect of the issue, it is perhaps worthwhile to consider briefly the methodology and results of the articles based on foreign data. Insofar as business cycles and lagged responses to policy actions are universal phenomena (among developed economies), the conclusions of such studies may be quite relevant to the domestic question. Furthermore, studies dealing with the Canadian experience may be particularly apropos. As Keith A.J. Hay observed in the introduction to his article concerning monetary policy lags in Canada:

> The near coincidence of most cyclical turning points has reinforced the contention that Canada is highly sensitive to American economic fluctuations[51].

Hay's method was very much like that of Friedman and Schwartz; he used a 7-month moving average of the rate of change in the money stock (currency in the hands of the public plus all commercial bank deposits except those held by the federal government) to identify peaks and troughs in the money series. (These peaks and troughs served as indicators of the timing of monetary policy actions.) As indication of a response in economic activity, Canadian reference cycle turning points were used. The lead of the money series with respect to the turning points was 18 months between peaks and 12 months between troughs. Both were highly variable over the period treated (1877-1961).

An earlier study of Canadian data published by George Macesich in 1962[52] had given essentially the same results as Hay's study. Macesich, like Hay, was indebted to Milton Friedman for some of his theoretical framework and much of the methodology. For the period 1924 through 1958 he correlated fluctuations in the monthly rate of change in the Canadian money stock with peaks and troughs in economic activity as dated on basis of National Bureau of Economic Research criteria. Not surprisingly, Macesich discovered long lags: the money series as defined led economic activity an average of 16.6 months at peaks and 6.6 months at troughs. Furthermore, he found that the lags at both peaks and troughs were so highly variable as to make it impossible to predict economic fluctuations from money stock growth rate fluctuations. Macesich concluded that discretionary monetary policy was too unreliable to be of great value as a discretionary economic stabilizer.

In 1966, A.A. Walters published the results of an empirical analysis of data for the United Kingdom[53] which was designed primarily to "examine statistically the relationship between the stock of money and money income"[54]. The data used were primarily yearly although some regressions using quarterly data were done for "recent" years. Walters' technique was to use lagged regressions, linear in the logarithms, to estimate the elasticity of nominal income, prices, and interest rates each with respect to the money supply. Using single-equation models and yearly data he estimated that the average lag between a change in the quantity of money and the initial effect on the economy was 6 months, that about one-half of the effect would be realized by the end of the first year, and that the balance of the effect would have occurred before the end of the second year. It seemed clear in Walters' view that the long-run elasticity of nominal income with respect to the money supply was unity prior to World War II (although he placed little confidence in the lag estimates because of the use of yearly data), but the more recent period was an enigma. In an attempt to explain why the earlier period appeared to conform to the traditional monetary model while the more recent period appeared to fit the Keynesian model best, he constructed a three-equation simultaneous-equation model and tested it in several forms. Using logarithms of the data and two-stage least squares for parameter estimation Walters was unable to produce empirical support for his theoretical constructs. The article was not policy oriented, but it may be safely concluded that Walters would advocate considerable additional study before any substantial modifications to the system are made.

An interesting variation of the usual monetary lag pattern is Arnold Harberger's study of inflation in Chile[55]. The purpose of the project was to determine the connection, if any, between the growth rate of the money supply and the rising price level in Chile during the period from 1939 through 1958. Harberger recognized at the outset that the effects of changes in the money stock were neither immediate nor discrete, so his first problem was to study the lag in effect of money stock changes on various price indexes. Using yearly data he found that including lagged values of the money stock beyond the current year and the preceding one added nothing to the explanatory power of his linear regression. Using quarterly data Harberger regressed percentage changes in the price level (both wholesale and consumer indexes) on percentage changes in the money supply for the preceding 6 months and, as a second independent variable, the same monetary measure for the period from 6 to 12 months earlier. He discovered that the coefficient of the independent variable for the most recent 6-month period was about double that of the second. From this he concluded that the coefficients for earlier observations would follow the same pattern; thus he created parameter constraints for the lagged values of the monetary variable. The parameters imply that about one-half of the effect of money stock changes on the price level will have been realized within 6 months, three-fourths within the first year, seven-eights after 18 months, and after 2 years no significant effect will remain. Although the study did not deal specifically with the effects of monetary policy actions on economic activity in general, it is relevant to the issue because of the econometric methods and because of the relationship of price fluctuations to real and nominal income.

Thomas Mayer[56] cited a Canadian study by Harry G. Johnson and John W.L. Winder which undertook to measure the lags in effect of monetary policy in Canada. Their technique was linear regression analysis and they apparently used two different models, the one in which they placed more confidence yielding a 6-month to 1-year lag, the other much longer, perhaps over 2 years.

Econometric Models

Econometric forecasting models usually have some monetary policy lag incorporated into the structural equations and, accordingly, most of the builders of these models have made statistical estimates of the lag. The Wharton model[57], for example, forecasts change in a number of variables on the basis of empirically derived patterns of effects of changes in exogenous variables. Two of these policy variables are controlled by the central bank: the discount rate and the level of free reserves. The schedule of effects of changes in the ratio of free reserves to required reserves on gross national product reflects that the lag is distributed over a long period beginning in the third quarter after the policy action and reaching a peak in the seventh quarter[58]. The model's quarterly and yearly forecasts are made on this assumption.

In 1964, R.R. Rhomberg published the results of an econometric study for Canada in which he had estimated the time path of responses to fiscal and monetary policy actions of unadjusted gross national product[59]. The basic purpose of the study was to compare the effects of fiscal and monetary policy under the assumptions of free versus fixed exchange rates. Using changes in the money stock as the monetary policy proxy, Rhomberg developed a distributed lag in the effect on the gross national product which reflected some response after one quarter, a gradual build-up to a peak in about the ninth quarter, then a gradual decline in effect[60]. Although substantial effects were reflected during the first year, the influence of sizable changes in the money stock appeared to persist for several additional quarters.

A particularly important econometric model from the standpoint of monetary policy lags is the study reported by Frank de Leeuw and Edward Gramlich in the January 1968 issue of the *Federal Reserve Bulletin*[61]. It is important because it had "as its major purpose the quantification of monetary policy and its effect on the economy"[62]. Having constructed a three-sector model (financial, fixed-investment, and consumption-inventory), de Leeuw and Gramlich simulated various possible policy actions to determine the timing and amplitude of the effect of each. A $½ billion step increase in unborrowed reserves proved to be a powerful policy action but it was a year before the really significant impact on gross national product occurred. After 3 years, the model predicted, gross national product would have risen by over $11 billion; but half of the net increase would have occurred after the sixth quarter. This led de Leeuw and Gramlich to conclude that "monetary policy is difficult to use as a stabilization device"[63].

Summary

Reference to an empirical study of the lag in effect of monetary policy that appeared in the May 1970 issue of the *Quarterly Journal of Economics* will facilitate a review of the issues[64]. In the study, William E. Gibson argued that changes in the money stock (such changes reflecting exclusively the effects of monetary policy actions) influence, first, the prices of government securities, then, through arbitrage, interest rates generally. The effects of money stock fluctuations on market interest rates were categorized by Gibson as of three main types: liquidity, income, and price expectations. The liquidity effect is the result of the efforts of wealth holders to reestablish the equilibrium of the demand for and supply of money after a policy-originated change in the level of the stock of money. The falling interest rates imply that the rates of return on capital will exceed the market rate for a time and there will be a resulting increase in the production of capital goods, which would raise income directly at first, then indirectly through the multiplier effect. This sequence Gibson labeled "the income effect." If the increase in income brought about by the falling interest rates is primarily nominal, i.e., if prices rise substantially, then people may be prompted to expect price rises in the future; this is Gibson's "price-expectations effect." (As lenders anticipate inflation they raise interest rates to compensate.)

Gibson theorized that the liquidity effects of monetary policy would predominate in the very short run; then, as changing interest rates affected investment, the income effect would become more significant. The price-expectations effect, which, like the income effect, tends to counter the liquidity effect on interest rates, may come soon after monetary policy changes and, if strong enough, even maintain interest rates at or above the prepolicy action levels.

To determine the timing of the effects of monetary changes on interest rates and nominal income, Gibson first regressed three interest rate proxies on the rate of change in the monthly series of money stock. Next, he regressed the rate of change in the interest rate series on the derivative of the rate of change in the money stock with respect to time. The second procedure produced clearer patterns of coefficients as well as statistically significant negative coefficients for the first few periods.

One conclusion of Gibson's study was that there is "an immediate and significant negative effect [of monetary fluctuations] on market interest rates"[65]. He pointed out, however, that only after from 3 to 9 months do the coefficients become positive, indicating, according to the theoretical construct presented in the article, that the income and price-expectations effects had reversed the trend in interest rates. The implication was that the effect on income had occurred within a 3 to 9 month period after the original monetary change.

Gibson cautioned against the use of interest rates as an indicator of the thrust of monetary policy or of its effect. "Monetary acceleration will indeed cause interest rates to fall, but the acceleration will also soon thereafter cause rates to rise again as the rate of change of income adjusts"[66]. His conclusion had policy implications: if the effects of monetary changes occur quickly and reliably, then the chances of using monetary policy effectively for stabilization purposes appear very good.

If policy were made on a purely democratic basis, the 17 studies which have been discussed would constitute a majority vote for abandoning discretionary monetary policy. A significant majority have concluded that the lag in effect of monetary policy is long, hence that stabilization efforts of the Federal Open Market Committee are likely to be ineffective or even counterproductive. This position may be correct, but the evidence submitted thus far is inconclusive. It will be argued that the outcomes of the analyses mentioned above were strongly influenced by the assumptions (explicit and implicit), by the selection of data, and by the methodologies employed. A systematic approach to measuring the lag makes it necessary to challenge these assumptions, methodologies, and data. Most of the studies in question have been criticized in detail in the literature, hence it would be redundant to develop separate commentary for each in this study. The criticism which is relevant to this study is of a more general nature; it is presented in the next chapter as a background and basis for the proposal of a nonparametric approach.

Notes

1. Milton Friedman, "The Role of Monetary Policy," *American Economic Review,* vol. 58 (March 1968), p. 16.

2. Henry C. Simons, "Rule Versus Authority in Monetary Policy," in Fredrich A. Lutz and Lloyd W. Mints, eds., *Readings in Monetary Theory* (Homewood, Ill.: Richard D. Irwin, Inc., 1951), pp. 337-368; originally published in the *Journal of Political Economy,* vol. 44 (February 1936), pp. 1-30.

3. Milton Friedman, "A Monetary and Fiscal Framework for Economic Stability," in *ibid.,* p. 381; originally published in the *American Economic Review,* vol. 38 (June 1948), pp. 245-264.

4. Milton Friedman, *Essays in Positive Economics* (Chicago: University of Chicago Press, 1953), pp. 117-132.

5. $$\begin{aligned}\sigma_z^2 &= E\,[Z-E\,(Z)\,]^2 = E\{[X-E\,(X)\,] + [Y-E\,(Y)\,]\}^2 \\ &= E\,[X-E\,(X)\,]^2 + E\,[Y-E\,(Y)\,]^2 + 2E\{[X-E\,(X)\,] \\ &\quad \times [Y-E\,(Y)\,]\} \\ &= \sigma_X^2 + \sigma_Y^2 + 2r_{XY}\sigma_X\sigma_Y\end{aligned}$$

   Note that if X and Y are independent, $r = 0$ and the last term disappears.

6. Milton Friedman, *The Optimum Quantity of Money and Other Essays* (Chicago: Aldine Publishing Co., 1969), p. 186. Hereafter referred to as *Optimum Quantity of Money;* originally published in Joint Economic Committee, "The Supply of Money and Changes in Prices and Output," 85th Cong., 2d Sess. (Washington, D.C.: Government Printing Office, 1958).

7. Milton Friedman, *A Program for Monetary Stability* (New York: Fordham University Press, 1959), p. 95.

8. *Ibid.,* p. 96.

9. *Ibid.,* p. 98.

10. J.M. Culbertson, "Friedman on the Lag in Effect of Monetary Policy," *Journal of Political Economy,* vol. 68 (December 1960), pp. 617-621.

11. Milton Friedman, "The Lag in Effect of Monetary Policy," *Journal of Political Economy,* vol. 69 (October 1961), p. 457.

12. *Ibid.,* p. 459.

13. Milton Friedman and Gary S. Becker, "A Statistical Illusion in Judging Keynesian Models," *Journal of Political Economy,* vol. 65 (February 1957), p. 74.

14. Friedman, *Optimum Quantity of Money,* p. 163; originally published as "Price, Income, and Monetary Changes in Three Wartime Periods," *American Economic Review,* vol. 42 (May 1952), pp. 612-625.

15. Friedman, *Optimum Quantity of Money,* p. 172.

16. Friedman, *Optimum Quantity of Money,* p. 190; originally published by Milton Friedman and Anna J. Schwartz as "Money and Business Cycles," *Review of Economics and Statistics,* vol. 45, no. 1, part 2: Supplement (February 1963).

17. Milton Friedman and Anna J. Schwartz, *A Monetary History of the United States, 1867-1960* (Princeton: Princeton University Press, 1963), p. xxii.

18. *Ibid.,* p. xxi.

19. Friedman, "The Lag in Effect of Monetary Policy," p. 458.

20. *Ibid.*

21. *Ibid.*, p. 460.

22. Milton Friedman and David Meiselman, "The Relative Stability of Monetary Velocity and the Investment Multiplier in the United States, 1897-1958," in Commission on Money and Credit, *Stabilization Policies* (Englewood Cliffs, N.J.: Prentice-Hall, Inc., 1963), p. 203.

23. Friedman, *Optimum Quantity of Money*, p. 187.

24. Beryl Sprinkel, "Monetary Growth as a Cyclical Predictor," *Journal of Finance*, vol. 14 (September 1959), pp. 333-346.

25. *Ibid.*, p. 337.

26. Clark Warburton, "The Theory of Turning Points in Business Fluctuations," *Quarterly Journal of Economics*, vol. 64 (November 1950), p. 544.

27 *Ibid.*, pp. 548-549.

28. Clark Warburton, "Bank Reserves and Business Fluctuations," *Journal of the American Statistical Association*, vol. 43 (December 1948), pp. 547-558.

29. *Ibid.*, p. 549.

30. John Kareken and Robert M. Solow, "Lags in Monetary Policy," in Commission on Money and Credit, *Stabilization Policies* (Englewood Cliffs, N.J.: Prentice-Hall, Inc., 1963), pp. 14-96.

31. *Ibid.*, p. 3.

32. *Ibid.*, p. 26.

33. *Ibid.*, p. 2.

34. Thomas Mayer, "The Inflexibility of Monetary Policy," in Richard S. Thorn, ed., *Monetary Theory and Policy* (New York: Random House, 1966), pp. 594-627; originally published in *Review of Economics and Statistics*, vol. 50 (November 1958), pp. 358-374.

35. *Ibid.*, p. 595.

36. *Ibid.*, p. 595.

37. *Ibid.*

38. Leonall C. Anderson and Jerry L. Jordan, "Monetary and Fiscal Actions: A Test of Their Relative Importance in Economic

Stabilization," reprint from *Review,* Federal Reserve Bank of St. Louis, no. 34 (November 1968).

39. *Ibid.,* p. 11.

40. *Ibid.,* p. 16.

41. *Ibid.,* p. 22n.

42. *Ibid.,* p. 22.

43. Philip Cagan and Arthur Gandolfi, "The Lag in Monetary Policy as Implied by the Time Pattern of Monetary Effects on Interest Rates," *American Economic Review Papers and Proceedings,* vol. 59 (May 1969), pp. 277-284.

44. *Ibid.,* p. 280.

45. See Chart I, *ibid.,* p. 281.

46. J. Ernest Tanner, "Lags in the Effects of Monetary Policy: A Statistical Investigation," *American Economic Review,* vol. 59 (December 1969), pp. 794-805.

47. *Ibid.,* p. 798.

48. Donald P. Tucker, "Dynamic Income Adjustment to Money Supply Changes," *American Economic Review,* vol. 56 (June 1966), pp. 433-449.

49. Tanner, *op. cit.,* p. 803.

50. William R. Bryan, "Bank Adjustments to Monetary Policy: Alternative Estimates of the Lag," *American Economic Review,* vol. 57 (September 1967), pp. 855-864.

51. Keith A.J. Hay, "Money and Cycles in Post-Confederation Canada," *Journal of Political Economy,* vol. 75 (June 1967), p. 263.

52. George Macesich, "The Rate of Change in Money Stock as a Leading Canadian Indicator," *Canadian Journal of Economics and Political Science,* vol. 28 (August 1962), pp. 424-430.

53. A.A. Walters, "Monetary Multipliers in the United Kingdom 1880-1962," *Oxford Economic Papers,* vol. 18 (November 1966), pp. 270-283.

54. *Ibid.,* p. 270.

55. Arnold C. Harberger, "The Dynamics of Inflation in Chile," in Carl Christ *et al.*, eds., *Measurement in Economics* (Stanford, Calif.: Stanford University Press, 1963), pp. 219-250.

56. Thomas Mayer, "The Lag in Effect of Monetary Policy: Some Criticisms," *Western Economic Journal,* vol. 7 (September 1965), pp. 324-342.

57. Michael Evans and Lawrence Klein, *The Wharton Econometric Forecasting Model* (Philadelphia: Wharton School of Finance and Commerce, University of Pennsylvania, 1967).

58. *Ibid.,* p. 65.

59. R.R. Rhomberg, "A Model of the Canadian Economy under Fixed and Flexible Exchange Rates," *Journal of Political Economy,* vol. 72 (February 1964), pp. 1-31.

60. *Ibid.,* p. 22.

61. Frank de Leeuw and Edward Gramlich, "The Federal Reserve–MIT Econometric Model," *Federal Reserve Bulletin,* vol. 54 (January 1968), pp. 11-40.

62. *Ibid.,* p. 11.

63. *Ibid.,* p. 27.

64. William E. Gibson, "The Lag in Effect of Monetary Policy on Income and Interest Rates," *Quarterly Journal of Economics,* vol. 84 (May 1970), pp. 288-300.

65. *Ibid.,* p. 298.

66. *Ibid.*

3

Alternative Approaches to the Statistical Analysis of Time Lags

Background

In the preceding chapter it was alleged that the conclusions concerning the lag in effect of monetary policy based on the parametric studies cited were strongly influenced by the assumptions (explicit and implicit) of each. The purpose of this chapter is to explain the bases for that contention, both generally in relation to the statistical techniques used and specifically from the standpoint of economic theory. Before proceeding with the discussion, however, it seems appropriate to emphasize the fact that this chapter is not intended to be a condemnation of the use of parametric statistics in the analysis of time series data. Rather, it is an argument in favor of using distribution-free tests whenever necessary due to data limitations or whenever possible because of the generality of the conclusions.

The Problems of Estimating the Lags in Effects of Monetary Policy with Parametric Statistics

The following treatment of the application of statistical analysis to economic time series data is divided into four parts. The first section deals with the problems involved in using parametric statistics to estimate the lag in effect of monetary policy. Second, some theoretical objections are raised. Next, a suitable policy indicator is suggested. Finally, a brief discussion of distribution-free statistical methods follows.

The first issue with which any study of the lag in effect of monetary policy must deal is the identification of a suitable indicator of the timing of monetary policy decisions. Most of the studies reviewed have used fluctuations in some measure of the money stock as the basis for assigning dates to changes in monetary policy. It will be shown that changes in the money stock are not suitable indicators for such purposes and that the ultimately appropriate data are not adaptable to parametric analysis.

As an introduction to the distribution-free analysis which is to be proposed, it will be postulated, for purposes of argument, that the money stock series is an accurate indicator of the timing of monetary policy. It will then be argued that, even under this restrictive assumption, the conclusions of a parametric study are questionable, the factors tending to invalidate the study being the assumptions underlying any parametric analysis, the effects of data aggregation, and the effects of averaging time series data over successive periods. The first objection could be overcome by simply eliminating the strong assumptions concerning the underlying distributions, but the two remaining problems are inherent in the data. It follows, then, that the nominal data which do accurately reflect policy timing must be used and, therefore, that the analysis must be of the nonparametric type.

On the assumption that fluctuations in the money stock (measured in some way) are accurate indicators of the timing of monetary policy changes, parametric methods can be employed to determine the length and variability of the lag in effect of monetary policy on macroeconomic activity (represented by some aggregate series such as gross national product or net national product). In fact, the use of parametric statistics allows the analyst to measure not only the timing but also the magnitude of the influence of the independent variable(s) on the dependent variable and to establish confidence limits for his estimates of the underlying structural relationships; hence, parametric statistics should be used whenever they are applicable. A discussion of the conditions under which parametric tests are appropriate will help to point up some of the problems encountered in any attempt to draw statistical inferences from time series data.

One of the most common statistical tools used by economists is regression analysis – especially linear regression analysis. This method involves the utilization of sample data to generate estimates of population parameters and residual variations from predicted values. A simple multivariate linear regression equation might be expressed in the form

$$Y = \alpha + \beta_1 X_1 + \beta_2 X_2 + \cdots + \beta_n X_n + \epsilon \qquad (3\text{-}1)$$

which is a general mathematical statement of the relationship between the dependent variable Y and the independent variables X_i ($i=1, 2, \cdots, n$). The α's and β's are constants which specify the degree of influence of the independent variables on the dependent variable, and ϵ is the variation in Y which is not associated with changes in the independent variables specified.

When the estimate of the parameters is based on time series data, observed values of Y are regressed on observed values of X_i for the period selected. Depending on the theoretical construct to be tested, the observed values of the independent variables may be matched with values of Y for the same period, earlier periods, or both. Determination of the estimates of the parameters is accomplished by the application of the least-squares criterion, a process which fits an equation to a set of sample points "such that the sum of the squares of the deviations of the sample points from the fitted line or curve is a minimum"[1]. The important point is that the process itself requires certain assumptions about the data and the relationships postulated.

First, the simple mathematical operations involved demand that the data in question may have been measured at least at the interval level. This means, essentially, that the measurement scale is such that the ratios of differences of any two intervals are independent of the scale and of the arbitrary zero point. Numerical values assigned to basically categorical groupings, for example, would not qualify; such data are nominal. Similarly, cardinal values assigned to ordinal data (data for which it is known only that A > B > C) are not conformable for addition, multiplication, and division[2].

Second, the specification of the regression parameters is a logical corollary of the assumption that the residuals are normally distributed. In this sense it could be said that regression analysis is not only a process for generating estimates of α and β but also, what is equally important, a method of determining residual variations from estimated values of Y, given a set of parameter values[3]. Under the usual assumptions the distribution of the residuals is one-dimensional regardless of the number of parameters included in the equation. While meaningful economic analysis involves a measure of abstraction, this assumption of the regression requires that all related variables be included; otherwise the excluded variables will operate on the error term in such a manner as to invalidate the assumption of a one-dimensional, normally distributed error term with zero mean[4].

Another restricting assumption which is closely related to the one just discussed is that of homoscedasticity; not only must the residuals be normally distributed but also the variance must be the same for all possible points on the regression. In the case of a bivariate regression the assumption of homoscedasticity means simply that the standard error of estimate is constant all along the line of regression. If the regression is multivariate, an analogous assumption is made: "for any point on a regression it is possible to compute a standard deviation of the deviations from the regression . . . [which is] constant for all points on the regression locus . . ."[5]. It is intuitively obvious that this particular assumption is an especially stringent one; what is not obvious is just how serious a doubt would be placed on the confidence limits of a regression estimate if the assumption should prove to be unrealistic.

Identification of a suitable indicator of the timing of monetary policy actions was mentioned as an empirical difficulty. There is another identification problem of a statistical nature. It is not enough that a system of equations be mathematically complete in the sense that it has as many equations as unknowns. Estimation of structural coefficients from sample data requires some prior empirical or a priori knowledge of some of the parameters or, perhaps, of some of the exogenous variables[6]. In the present instance if

$$M^d = \alpha + \beta Y + \epsilon \tag{3-2}$$

and

$$M^s = \gamma + \delta Y + \zeta \tag{3-3}$$

where M^d = the demand for money, M^s = the money stock, Y = some measure of income, α, β, γ, and δ are structural parameters, and ϵ and ζ are the error terms, it would be impossible to estimate the parameters from sample data of income and the money supply without considerably more information than provided in Eqs. (3-2) and (3-3).

For example, if it could be assumed that ϵ and ζ are independent, then knowledge of the coefficient of Y in either equation would make it possible to obtain an unbiased estimate of the other coefficient through linear regression. This is true because, under the assumption of independence, the equation estimated would necessarily produce a simultaneous solution with the equation with known parameters such that the error terms would sum to zero. If, on the other hand, the error terms ϵ and ζ are not known to be independent, then there is an unlimited number of sets of parameters which could fit the sample data. Equating M^d and M^s only produces:

$$Y = \frac{\gamma - \alpha}{\beta - \delta} \tag{3-4}$$

This means that the reduced form coefficient is a combination of all four structural parameters and it is impossible to determine specific values for each.

Some techniques have been developed for dealing with underidentified systems, but the methods require, in turn, additional information and assumptions which are not always readily available and reliable. One of the studies reviewed in Chap. 2 utilized the two stage least-squares technique to deal with the identification problem[7].

A least-squares assumption which can be particularly troublesome when the data are from a time series is the supposition that no autocorrelation exists in the data, i.e., that the error term of any given observation is independently distributed with respect to any other error term. It is especially important to note that "regression models fitted to economic time series data almost always evidence some degree of stochastic dependence between successive values of the error term"[8]. Not only does autocorrelation occur in time series due to the usual trends and cyclical fluctuations; it can be a reflection of a host of natural or political factors operating in an economy (hurricanes, floods, droughts, wars). In fact, autocorrelation may be introduced into a time series by the application of commonly-used adjusting and smoothing techniques[9]. Again, the question is: Just how serious is a violation of the assumption of nonautocorrelation? (Tests have been developed for determining the degree of autocorrelation in a series, and there are techniques for eliminating the influence of autocorrelation.)

The process by which one difficulty is obviated may, however, give rise to other complications. Suppose, for example, that the assumption of a normally distributed residual is invalidated because of a variable which has been omitted from the equation; the solution may be, simply, to add the variable in question. However, if the variable added should prove to be correlated with one or more of the variables in the original equation (a commonly observed phenomenon in time series analysis), then a form of single-equation bias may be the result.

Multicollinearity is the name given to the

general problem which arises when some or all of the explanatory

> variables in a relation are so highly correlated one with another that it becomes very difficult, if not impossible, to disentangle their separate influences and obtain a reasonably precise estimate of their relative effects[10].

So it is quite possible that a procedure for solving one problem may give rise to another.

All except one of the studies reviewed in Chap. 2[11] incorporate at least some of the assumptions which have been discussed above. As has been mentioned, techniques have been developed for solving the various problems which arise in the course of any econometric study; certain adjustments can be made to deal with serial correlation, multicollinearity, heteroscedasticity, simultaneous equations bias, and so forth. However, if more than one of these difficulties should arise in a given analysis, the solution of one may complicate the other:

> Thus, if both problems arise simultaneously, we cannot treat them by somehow adding together the treatments appropriate for the cases in isolation; instead we require a properly developed, integrated treatment, designed for the case at hand, but this is not yet available[12].

Obviously, to abandon all attempts at econometric analysis would eliminate any possibility of solving economic problems by such methods—a result which most economists would find unacceptable. But to proceed as if there were no problem with the data or the assumptions would tend to produce and perpetuate unfounded conclusions. As one econometrician wrote:

> The heroic assumptions whereby econometric arguments proceed (specifying restrictions and empirical definitions of concepts) require continual examination. . . .
>
> To succeed, would-be econometricians must anticipate and surmount a veritable parade of unpleasant problems[13].

Economists should agree, then, that parametric statistical analysis of economic time series data, in spite of all of the implied problems, is better than no analysis at all. Nevertheless, there may be certain types of economic estimation which are peculiarly unsuited for time series analysis. Estimation of time lags in adjustment between successive equilibria may be a case in point.

In Chap. 2 it was reported that William R. Bryan had collected microeconomic data for the purpose of estimating one phase of the monetary lag and upon aggregating the data found that the lag estimate had increased substantially. He also produced successively longer estimates of the lag by averaging the original weekly data into monthly, quarterly, then yearly periods. Although Bryan's study was based on a small sample (19 banks from the Eighth Federal Reserve District), it does suggest that data aggregation and averaging may introduce bias into the lag estimates.

The conditions under which data aggregation can be considered consistent are, if anything, more stringent than the assumptions underlying the least-squares criterion[14]. For example, if microeconomic data are to be aggregated for use in a regression analysis as the basis for estimating macroeconomic parameters, then the behavioral assumptions underlying the microeconomic relationships postulated must be consistent with the relationships reflected in the macroeconomic model. The process of expansion of bank credit described in Chap. 1 can be used to illustrate the point.

Assume a closed economy with a central banking system requiring fractional reserves equal to r. Assume that all banks seek to maximize profits and, further, that the system is in equilibrium in the sense that each bank is satisfied, under the prevailing conditions with respect to opportunities and costs, with its level of excess reserves (or borrowings). Finally, assume that all increases in excess reserves are considered unwanted excess reserves and that there are no leakages to currency or time deposits. If banks adjust to increases in unwanted excess reserves by lending the entire amount of each increase, then the behavior of an individual bank can be described as follows:

$$\Delta L = (1-r)\ \Delta D \tag{3-5}$$

where ΔL is the change in loans outstanding and ΔD the assumed change in primary deposits. A bank receiving a deposit as a result of an open market purchase of government securities by the Federal Reserve would expand loans outstanding by the amount of the deposit less the product of the deposit multiplied by the reserve requirement. Thus, Eq. (3-5) describes the reaction of one bank to a deposit increase initiated by Federal Reserve open market policy action. But the credit expansion, under the present assumptions, does not end at that point. The loan (or loans) made by the bank receiving the initial deposit becomes a deposit (deposits) in another bank (banks). The total expansion of loans for a given number n of stages in the sequence is

$$\Delta L_n = \Delta D \sum_{i=1}^{n} (1-r)^i \tag{3-6}$$

Note that the function is exponential (not linear) and in the limit asymptotically approaches

$$\Delta L_n = \Delta D \frac{1}{r} \tag{3-7}$$

Clearly, then, the macroeconomic effects of open market operations as described by Eqs. (3-6) and (3-7) are different from the microeconomic effects implied by Eq. (3-5) and the assumptions underlying each are different. The individual bank must act upon the assumption that the total deposit created by the loan which has been made to a client will be withdrawn almost immediately (ignoring the effects of possible compensating balance agreements). On the other hand, it is obvious that the banking system as a whole, given the assumptions listed, cannot lose deposits created by derivative loans.

It has been shown that consistency in aggregation requires that

> knowledge of the 'macro-relation' (the function relating the aggregates), and the values of the aggregate independent variables, would lead to the same value of the aggregate dependent variable as a

> knowledge of the micro-relations and of the values of the individual independent variables[15].

Moreover, in the case of macro and micro functions of credit expansion the inconsistency is especially critical from the standpoint of timing. The expansion process itself implies that the aggregate effect reaches a maximum subsequent to the maximum micro effect.

Superficially it may seem that the aggregate behavior, when determined by summation of individual units, should always reflect the same structural relationships as the individual units. Actually, this outcome can occur only under highly special conditions. Consider, for example, the fact that country banks tend to maintain higher excess reserves than do reserve city banks in the United States. It is conceivable, then, that two banks with identical resources may allocate those resources among alternatives in entirely different ways, depending upon the preferences of the individual banks. Is it possible that such an asymmetry in funds allocation might produce inconsistency in the macro relationships when aggregated? A well-known argument from price theory provides the answer[16].

Two banks holding identical amounts of funds for allocation between two alternatives, say between excess reserves and interest-bearing investments, may have liquidity preference patterns such that one holds more excess reserves than the other. If the data from the banks were aggregated, the liquidity budget would be just doubled and the ratio of funds devoted to the two uses would be the average of the two individual ratios. This funds allocation would represent a macroeconomic equilibrium. From the position of equilibrium a change in the relative yields of the two alternatives would produce a change in the amount of funds allocated to one or both of the uses.

In Slutsky's consumer budget analysis, the change from one combination of goods to another is divided into two parts: the income effect and the substitution effect. Under the usual assumptions of utility analysis, the substitution effect can only be negative; the maximizing consumer will substitute some of the good whose price has fallen for some of the other good. The income effect, on the other hand, may be positive, negative, or zero, depending on the type of good in question (normal, inferior, or neutral). If the income effect is positive and absolutely larger than the substitution effect, then the total effect of a price decline in one good will be that less of that good and more of the other will be consumed. The relationships presented in Slutsky's consumer budget analysis are precisely the same as those described in connection with the two banks.

The income effect in the consumer analysis is the change in consumption of the two goods which occurs as a result of the fact that the consumer is actually wealthier in real terms after a price decrease in one of the goods even though his money income has not changed. Similarly, in the heterogenous-banks example the increase in yield of one of the two alternative allocations of the liquidity funds produces an income effect as well as a substitution effect. Now with reference to the aggregate equilibrium reached after the change in yield of one of the alternatives in question, the income effect can be eliminated, as in Slutsky's analysis, by reducing the total amount of aggregate funds available for the liquidity accounts described to the level at which it would be just possible for the two banks to hold precisely the same total aggregated quantities of the two types of liquid assets as they had held before the change in relative yields. This means that the remaining substitution effect will insure that the quantity of the asset whose yield has risen will be greater, and that of the other smaller. The direction of movement of the aggregate equilibrium is determinate.

Consistent disaggregation of the funds available for allocation to the two liquid alternatives (after the downward adjustment for the income effect has been made) requires that the total amount be divided equally between the two banks. This being done, each bank will move from its original equilibrium to a new equilibrium which is consistent with its changed allotment of funds. It is altogether possible for each bank, without violating any of the assumptions of the analysis, to adjust in such a manner that their aggregated position will reflect a positive substitution effect

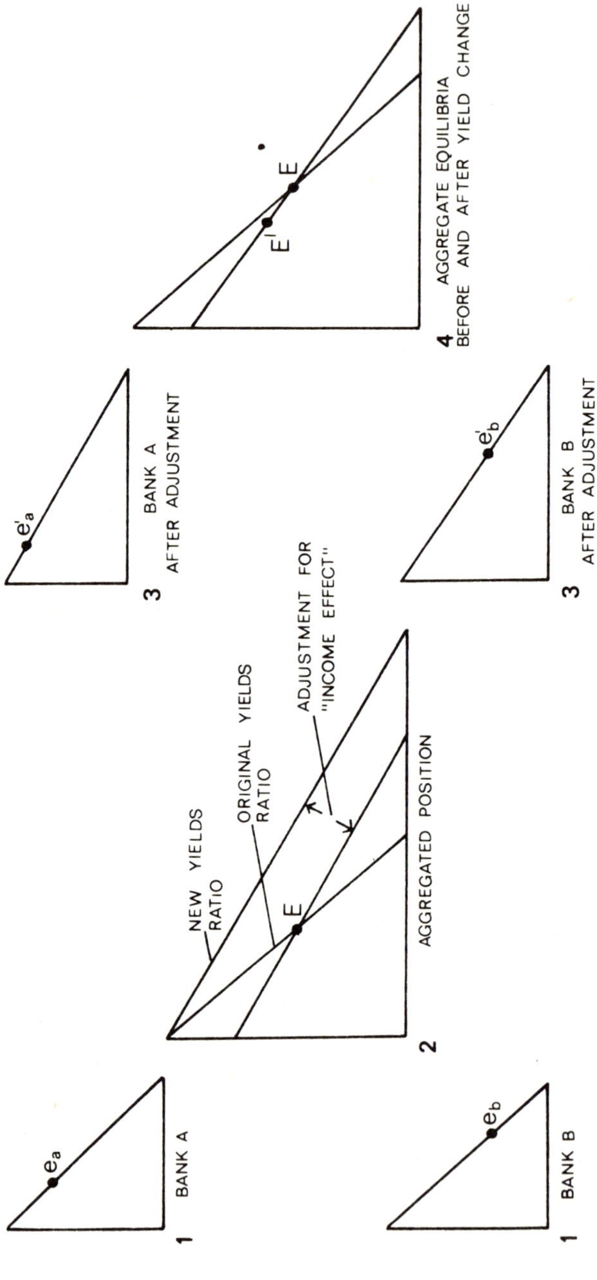

FIG. 3-1. Effects of inconsistent data aggregation.

(cf. Fig. 3-1). In indifference analysis this would mean that the aggregate indifference curves had crossed. In the general sense it means that, in the macro case, the decision units would have chosen a combination of alternatives which they had previously rejected.

Aggregation of micro data for the present lag analysis is, therefore, inappropriate. The general requirements for consistent aggregation are not met; the timing relationships with respect to the process by which bank credit expands are different in the macro and micro contexts; and the effects of aggregation on static equilibrium models are likely to produce inconsistencies (especially with micro data reflecting the allocation by banks of liquid funds).

Averaging time series data over successive periods is perhaps the most subtle and dangerous of the three techniques criticized in this chapter. It is damaging to any analysis of timing relationships because of the unpredictable effects on the frequency and regularity of peaks and troughs in the original series. The effects of such averaging may go undetected by the investigator because many of the series which are used as original data have already been averaged one time or more before publication. Many analyses involving time series data may produce legitimate conclusions despite data averaging; an analysis of the lag in effect of monetary policy may not escape the distortion implied by the process.

The indicator of the timing (and magnitude) of monetary policy employed by most of the studies reviewed in the previous chapter was the money supply series as reported in the *Federal Reserve Bulletin.* (As explained previously, some studies include as a part of the money supply series all time deposits in commercial banks.) These monthly data are compiled from two sources. Most of the dollar value represents weekly averages of daily closing figures as reported by all Federal Reserve System member banks located in reserve cities. A much smaller portion of the total money supply—but reflecting a significant majority of the member banks of the Federal Reserve System—is derived from data reported by the so-called country banks (those not located in reserve cities). Until very recently country banks reported their average deposit-reserve positions only every two weeks.

It is not the purpose of this section to quibble about the difficulties involved in averaging four reporting dates in some months and five in others, or about the problems implied by combining series derived from reports submitted at different intervals. The criticism is much more basic and far more relevant to the issue of identifying the timing of changes in monetary policy. The general case was made by Eugen Slutsky in 1937[17]. His study was concerned with the effects of smoothing series by moving averages and the possibility of introducing artificial fluctuations into a series.

> His principal conclusion was that the construction of a cumulative sequence of moving averages, each computed as a moving average of the previous one starting from purely random numbers, will in certain cases produce series that converge on a pure sine curve[18].

Both the mathematical argument presented in Slutsky's article and the empirical results described by William R. Bryan (cf. Chap. 2) in his study of alternative lag estimates suggest that averaging time series data may obscure the very timing relationships in question. In Fig. 3-2, X(t) is a representation of a stationary stochastic series by a sine wave. If the ordinates of the function are considered observations of the magnitude of the deviations from trend of a continuous time series, then observations of the ordinate height at regular intervals can represent daily or weekly observations of the deviations of the money stock from its trend. If the number of observations to be averaged multiplied by the interval between observations is not a factor of the period of the function, then the derivative curve produced by plotting the averages will have a different period from the original sine wave. Thus the location of the peaks and troughs along the time continuum will not coincide with those of the original series. The lag between a given peak (or trough) of the original series and any given location on the time axis will be different from that of the derived curve. The dashed line in Fig. 3-2 designated Z(t), represents the curve produced by averaging ordinates. It is interesting to note that deviations of the derived series from the trend of the original series are also different.

The manner in which a series may be affected by averaging has been presented in terms such that the correspondence between that phenomenon and the effects of stabilization policy on income fluctuation as explained by Friedman[19] will be obvious. The present analysis involves three stochastic series: X(t) representing the fluctuations of the money stock in the absence of averaging, Y(t) representing the effects of the described averaging process on X(t), and Z(t) representing money stock fluctuations of the averaged series:

$$Z(t) = X(t) + Y(t) \tag{3-8}$$

If the variances of X and Z are indexes of the magnitude of the fluctuation of each about its mean, then the variance of Y, as Friedman pointed out, is an index to the magnitude of the effects of Y. If X and Y are dependent,

$$\delta_Z^{\,2} = \delta_X^{\,2} + \delta_Y^{\,2} + 2r_{XY}\delta_X\delta_Y \tag{3-9}$$

In this discussion r_{XY} must be considered a measure of the degree of synchronization of the effects of the averaging procedure with the fluctuations in the unaveraged series. If there were perfect positive correlation between X and Y (if r_{XY} were +1), then the timing of peaks and troughs would not be affected. If there were perfect negative correlation between X and Y (if $r_{XY} = -1$), then the timing of peaks and troughs would be affected differently depending on the relative magnitudes of $\delta_X^{\,2}$ and $\delta_Y^{\,2}$. The timing relationship would be reversed if $\delta_Y^{\,2} > \delta_X^{\,2}$. If $\delta_Y^{\,2} = \delta_X^{\,2}$, the peaks and troughs would be eliminated. Only under the special circumstances in which $\delta_Y^{\,2} < \delta_X^{\,2}$ would the peaks and troughs in the averaged series be located on the time continuum coincident with those of the original series. Hence, two special cases would produce the same timing relationships in the averaged series and the original one.

Consider the assumption of perfect correlation between X and Y. Clearly, averaging can only reduce the amplitude of the fluctuations in the original series X(t). It follows from this observation that

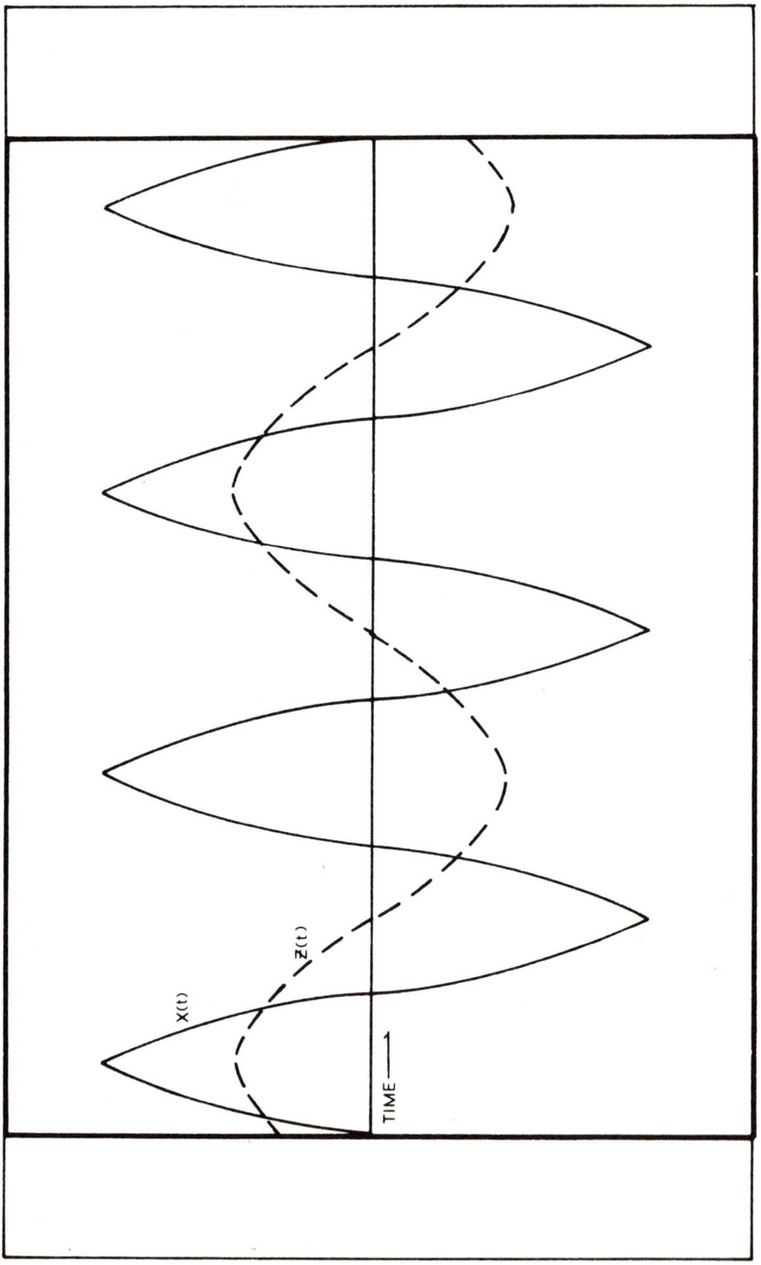

FIG. 3-2. Effects of averaging time series data.

$$\frac{\delta_Z^{\ 2}}{\delta_X^{\ 2}} < 1 \tag{3-10}$$

and from (3-9) that

$$r_{XY} < -\frac{1}{2}\frac{\delta_Y}{\delta_X} \tag{3-11}$$

But since δ_Y and δ_X are both necessarily positive, Eq. (3-11) implies that r_{XY} is negative; the assumption of perfect positive correlation between X and Y is inconsistent with Eq. (3-10). Therefore, if the averaging process is to produce a series with timing identical to X(t), X and Y must be perfectly negatively correlated ($r_{XY} = -1$).

Theoretical Objections to the Use of Money Stock Fluctuations as an Indicator of the Timing of Monetary Policy Actions

The use of fluctuations in a money stock series as an indicator of the timing of monetary policy decisions has been criticized on statistical grounds. There are theoretical objections as well. Implicit in the approach are the assumptions: (a) that the monetary authorities have immediate and absolute control over the level of the nominal money supply, (b) that they exercise that control continuously and exclusively for purposes of macroeconomic stabilization, and (c) that economic stability is never in conflict with other national goals such as full employment, sustainable growth, price stability, and balance-of-payments equilibrium. These assumptions are not just unrealistic in the sense that they do not accurately reflect reality; they are positively damaging to the study.

The discussion of the expansion of bank credit in Chap. 1 is sufficient to indicate that the linkage between the tools of monetary policy and the effect on the money supply is loose and only approximate. If the Federal Open Market Committee should instruct the Open Market Manager to increase the stock of money from one specific level to another by purchasing government securities (an unlikely instruction), the precise formula by which the order could be executed is simply not available. The reaction of bankers to changes in their reserves, the preferences of the public concerning the employment of liquid funds, and a host of unmanaged factors which influence the level of reserves concurrently determine the level of the money stock along with the factors managed by the Federal Reserve. Ultimate power to determine the level of reserves and the money stock rests with the Federal Reserve, but the control is neither precise nor immediate.

The assumption that the monetary authorities exercise control over the supply of money continuously and exclusively for the purpose of economic stabilization is similarly unrealistic. A casual reading of the minutes of the meetings of the Federal Open Market Committee reveals that other matters are considered. For example, the Federal Reserve generally supports Treasury funding operations so as to prevent disruption of the money market and to minimize the federal government's debt maintenance costs. During such periods the open market operations of the Federal Reserve may appear to be procyclical.

Stabilization in the sense implied by Friedman's formal analysis[20] is less important than other goals such as full employment. As has been observed, a scheme designed to "stabilize" the economy at a level where one-third of the labor force would be continuously unemployed would be unacceptable[21]. Stabilization policy must have as its primary objectives low unemployment, sustainable growth, price stability, and balance-of-payments equilibrium. Some fluctuation around a low level of unemployment is obviously more desirable than a stable high level of unemployment.

It has been shown that fluctuations in the level of the money stock are not accurate indicators of the timing of monetary policy actions. The argument has been based on a number of sufficient reasons both statistical and theoretical. Any measurement of the lag in effect of monetary policy should include as many of the components of the total lag (identified in Chap. 1) as possible so that underestimation will be minimized.

The recognition lag, that period between the occurrence of a need for action and the recognition of the need by the monetary authorities, may be positive, negative, or zero, depending upon the accuracy of the economic forecasts produced by the advisers to the policymaking body. Estimation of the recognition lag involves a separate evaluation of forecasting techniques and performance, and hence is a problem quite apart from the measurement of the lag in effect of monetary policy.

The time required for the monetary authorities to reach a decision to act (or not to act) is presumed to be quite short. The Federal Open Market Committee meets regularly every three weeks and, when the chairman deems it important, even more frequently. Some special sessions are conducted by telephone conference call; others, in Washington, D.C., with the voting members attending in person. Furthermore, the instructions issued to the manager of the trading desk in New York following each Open Market Committee meeting allow considerable latitude within which the manager may exercise his discretion depending upon economic developments. Decisions to act promptly when the need is obvious are certainly feasible and probably forthcoming.

The Monetary Lag from Policy Decision to Effect

It follows from the foregoing that the time period between the decision and the effect (however identified) is the monetary policy lag which is really meaningful. The time required for the instructions to reach the manager of the trading desk—certainly a short period in any case—is a part of the lag. The period between the initial attempt to pursue the policy through open market trading and the achievement of success by some set of criteria necessarily includes the effects of errors in judgment as well as the influence of unmanaged factors on the target variables. Such factors must be incorporated into any measurement of the lag in effect of monetary policy because of their obvious potential for influencing both the length and variability of the average estimate.

Assuming that the lag begins with the decision process, estimation of the lag must also begin there. But neither the consensus of the Committee nor the instruction to the open market manager is a quantitative prescription for action of a specific magnitude. The manager of the Federal Open Market Trading Desk (who attends all Federal Open Market Committee meetings) must decide what trading patterns to pursue in order to achieve the objectives identified by the most recent instruction from the Open Market Committee. Moreover, it is virtually certain that the manager's interpretation of his instructions will be influenced strongly by his knowledge of the entire proceedings of the meeting at which the instructions were formulated and approved. Any attempt to establish ratio measurements for such nominal data is almost certainly doomed.

The Appropriateness of Nonparametric Statistics for Measuring the Lag

The data which accurately establish the timing of monetary policy decisions are at best ordinal and perhaps only nominal, hence unsuitable for parametric analysis. The data by which general economic conditions are usually gauged are at least estimates of a ratio measurement and could be used under certain assumptions in a parametric study. The two sets of data can be combined in a nonparametric analysis designed to estimate the average length of the lag in effect of monetary policy. Obviously the conclusions of a study of this type will have certain limitations. No structural parameters can be estimated and, of course, the usual confidence limits for estimates of coefficients cannot be produced. But the question of timing can be evaluated and the conclusions will be completely general for the universe from which the sample was drawn. This study will produce such estimates of the total lag in effect of monetary policy plus probability ranges for the variation in effect based on a weak binomial assumption. A brief discussion of nonparametric statistics will establish the basis for the proposed study.

The adjectives "nonparametric" and "distribution-free" when used to modify the noun "statistics" are often used interchangeably. Actually, the line which divided parametric from nonparametric statistics is arbitrary and ill defined. All statistical tests require some assumptions about the data from which inferences are to be drawn; some types of tests require stronger assumptions than others. The assumptions enumerated above in connection with the application of the least-squares criterion are strong assumptions. Siegel made the distinction as follows:

> A nonparametric statistical test is a test whose model does not specify conditions about the parameters of the population from which the sample was drawn. Certain assumptions are associated with most nonparametric statistical tests, i.e., that the observations are independent and that the variable under study has underlying continuity, but these assumptions are fewer and much weaker than those associated with parametric tests[22].

By way of explanation of the subtle difference between nonparametric and distribution-free tests Bradley wrote:

> . . . a nonparametric test is one which makes no hypothesis about the value of a parameter in a statistical density function, whereas a distribution-free test is one which makes no assumptions about the precise form of the sampled population. The definitions are not mutually exclusive and a test can be both distribution-free and parametric. (For example the Sign test, which does not assume any exact shape for the sampled population of variate values tests the hypothesis that the parameter p of a binomial distribution has the value .5)[23].

This study will follow Bradley in using the terms synonymously to refer generally to distribution-free tests. This use is also consistent with that of Walsh who wrote: "the binomial distribution is considered to be of nonparametric interest even though it is of an elementary parametric form"[24].

Nonparametric statistics is a major field of study, a complete discussion of which is beyond the scope of this study. Chap. 4, accordingly, is a digression in which the nature of the empirical data which will be used to identify the timing and direction of monetary policy is discussed, thus establishing a basis for the formulation of a suitable nonparametric analysis.

Notes

1. Acheson J. Duncan, *Quality Control and Industrial Statistics* (Homewood, Ill.: Richard D. Irwin, Inc., 1965), p. 683. For a detailed explanation of the derivation of the regression equation by least squares, see pp. 881-883.

2. For an excellent discussion of the measurement requirement, see Sidney Siegel, *Nonparametric Statistics for the Behavioral Sciences* (New York: McGraw-Hill, 1956), pp. 21-34.

3. Edward J. Kane, *Economic Statistics and Econometrics* (New York: Harper and Row, 1968), pp. 351-352.

4. N.R. Draper and H. Smith, *Applied Regression Analysis* (New York: John Wiley and Sons, Inc., 1966), pp. 81-85.

5. Duncan, *op. cit.,* p. 725.

6. Ronald J. Wonnacott and Thomas H. Wonnacott, *Econometrics* (New York: John Wiley and Sons, Inc., 1970), pp. 172-180.

7. J. Ernest Tanner, "Lags in the Effects of Monetary Policy: A Statistical Investigation," *American Economic Review,* vol. 59 (December 1969), pp. 794-805.

8. Kane, *op. cit.,* pp. 359-360.

9. An example of spurious fluctuation introduced into a series by smoothing methods is the Slutsky-Yule effect; cf. Maurice G. Kendall and Alan Stuart, *The Advanced Theory of Statistics,* vol. 3 (New York: Hafner Publishing Company, 1966), p. 378ff.

10. J. Johnston, *Econometric Methods* (New York: McGraw-Hill, 1963), p. 201.

11. Thomas Mayer expressed some serious reservations concerning the value of time series analysis for the purpose of measuring the lag in effect of monetary policy and proceeded to employ, instead, estimates of the speed of adjustment in various sectors of the economy based primarily on expert testimony.

12. Johnston, *op. cit.,* p. 147.

13. Kane, *op. cit.,* p. 382.

14. For a detailed treatment of the statistical considerations involved, see H.A. John Green, *Aggregation in Economic Analysis* (Princeton, N.J.: Princeton University Press, 1964).

15. *Ibid.*, p. 35ff.

16. Eugen E. Slutsky, "On the Theory of the Budget of the Consumer," in George J. Stigler and Kenneth E. Boulding, eds., *Readings in Price Theory* (Homewood, Ill.: Richard D. Irwin, Inc., 1952), pp. 27-56.

17. Eugen Slutsky, "The Summation of Random Causes as a Source of Cyclic Processes," *Econometrica,* vol. 5 (April 1937), pp. 105-147.

18. Martin J. Bailey, *National Income and the Price Level* (New York: McGraw-Hill, 1962), p. 242.

19. Milton Friedman, *Essays in Positive Economics* (Chicago: The University of Chicago Press, 1953), pp. 117-132.

20. *Ibid.*

21. Thomas Mayer, *Monetary Policy in the United States* (New York: Random House, 1968), pp. 180-181.

22. Siegel, *op. cit.,* p. 31.

23. James V. Bradley, *Distribution-Free Statistical Tests* (Englewood Cliffs, N.J.: Prentice-Hall, Inc., 1968), p. 15.

24. John E. Walsh, *Handbook of Nonparametric Statistics,* vol. 1 (New York: D. Van Nostrand Company, Inc., 1962), p. 2.

4

Interpreting Federal Open Market Policy Decisions

Background

The Federal Open Market Committee, the body officially charged with the responsibility of formulating monetary policy involving the purchase and sale of United States government securities was organized in March 1936, pursuant to the Banking Act of 1935. As prescribed by the same law, minutes of each meeting of the Committee have been kept on record at the Federal Reserve Bank in Washington, D.C., since that time. These minutes contain, in addition to other important economic information, details of the policy decisions of the Committee and of the economic analyses on which those decisions were based. Before July 1964, these minutes were not available for public scrutiny and the actions of the Federal Open Market Committee were a mystery to all with the exception of a few high officials of the central bank.

On July 17, 1964, William McChesney Martin, Jr., then chairman of the Board of Governors of the Federal Reserve System and *ex officio* chairman of the Federal Open Market Committee, officially transmitted by letter to Dr. Wayne C. Grover, archivist of the United States, "the original signed copies of the minutes of the meetings of (1) the Federal Open Market Committee from 1936 to the end of 1960 and (2) its Executive Committee from March 1936 until June 1955 . . ."[1]. The letter of acknowledgement from the archivist indicated that the subject records would be picked up as soon as could be arranged; therefore, it can be assumed that these data were probably available at least by sometime in the early part of 1965[2]. At about the same time copies of the minutes were printed and bound and distributed to each Federal Reserve Bank and Branch. Furthermore, it was announced in the *Federal Reserve Bulletin* that "the National Archives is prepared to furnish copies of the records, at cost, to any interested parties . . ."[3]. The important point to be observed from the chronological details which have been related is that access to these valuable research documents was not available to most scholars until sometime after August 1964, and perhaps several months later. This fact alone could explain why the early analyses of the timing of the effects of monetary policy were parametric studies of time series data: better information was simply unavailable.

The records which were made available officially in 1964 extended only through December 1960. It is interesting to note that the minutes of the meetings for the year 1961 were not transferred to the Archives until sometime after June 23, 1967[4]. Between December 1961 and January 1967, there appears to have existed an information gap; neither minutes of Federal Open Market Committee meetings nor detailed statements of policy actions were available for this period. (Evaluation of the direction and intensity of open market policy decisions for this period must be based on the cryptic jargon of the directives to the manager of the trading desk in New York as recorded in the *Annual Reports* of the Board of Governors of the Federal Reserve System.) In 1967 details of policy actions were made readily available with a time delay:

> It is planned to release entries for policy actions taken subsequent to April 4, 1967, on a regular basis, approximately 90 days following the date of the meeting at which the corresponding policy actions were taken[5].

However, complete minutes of the meetings held since December 1961, are still unavailable. The reports of policy actions of the Committee are quite useful to a researcher in the field, but to interpret adequately the directives to the manager of the trading desk one must have available the same economic reports and discussions as the manager had at the time when he was devising precisely what trading patterns to follow. Therefore, analysis of the timing and intensity of monetary policy since December 1961, will necessarily be less precise.

The Basis for Selecting the Primary and Secondary Periods for Analysis

The 10-year period immediately preceding the Treasury-Federal Reserve Accord of March 1951, is also difficult to analyze from the standpoint of the effects of monetary policy as an instrument for the promotion of economic stability. During this period the Federal Reserve was committed to supporting Treasury funding operations by maintaining high prices on government securities through open market purchases. Countercyclical monetary policy was, accordingly, a secondary consideration (if a consideration at all). For the purpose of testing the relationship between countercyclical monetary policy and changes in the level of economic activity, therefore, the primary time period used in this study will be that decade from the Accord through the end of 1961. The secondary period will begin with January 1962, and extend through January 1970, when William McChesney Martin, Jr. was replaced by Professor Arthur Burns as chairman of the Board of Governors of the Federal Reserve System. The data for the second period are not complete and the interpretation of the Federal Open Market Committee directives are certainly less reliable than those for the preceding decade. Nevertheless, the basic thrust of monetary policy can generally be identified from the data available.

Goals of Monetary Policy

In analyzing the minutes of Open Market Committee meetings it must be borne in mind that the objectives of monetary policy may change over time[6]. In fact the actions by which the Committee attempts to pursue the same goal may be different at different times. These variations may be due to consideration of economic factors which alter the effects of monetary policy, or they may reflect differences in the consensus on economic theory of different committees. In any case it is useful to have a concrete statement of the goals of monetary policy by the Committee or their spokesman. Such a statement was provided by Chairman Martin in 1964:

> The purpose of the Federal Reserve System is to contribute—to the maximum extent that monetary policy can contribute—to the achievement of sustained high employment, stable values, and a rising standard of living for all Americans. It cannot of course achieve these goals alone, but it can contribute, and I can assure you that it is unreservedly dedicated to that end today[7].

It will be assumed, then, as a key to interpreting the minutes of the Open Market Committee meetings and the directives to the manager of the trading desk that the primary goals of monetary policy in the period in question were high employment, stable prices, real growth. (Referring to the period from 1951 to February 1970, the phrase "economic stabilization policy" will be used to designate those goals plus balance-of-payments equilibrium, which Chairman Martin clearly included as one of the objectives of monetary policy.)

Contents of the Minutes of the Meetings of the Federal Open Market Committee

During the course of reading several sets of minutes it becomes apparent that the key to their interpretation is to view the brief directive (the final item in most minutes) as a reminder to the trading desk manager of everything which has gone before. The detailed economic reports from the professional economists, the opinions of the Federal Reserve Bank presidents, the debate over the economic climate and the correct direction and intensity of policy, and the final vote of the Committee are "modifiers" of an injunction which appears at first glance to be almost hopelessly ambiguous and equivocating. For example:

> To implement this policy, System open market operations until the next meeting of the Committee shall be conducted with a view to maintaining on balance about the prevailing firm conditions in money and short-term credit markets; provided, however, that operations shall be modified if bank credit appears to be deviating significantly from current projections[8].

The two preceding paragraphs of this directive are a summary and conclusions based, presumably, on everything which transpired at the meeting. A further quotation from the same directive will illustrate the "modifier" relationship suggested above.

> In this situation, it is the policy of the Federal Open Market Committee to foster financial conditions conducive to the reduction of inflationary pressures, with a view to encouraging a more sustainable rate of economic growth and attaining reasonable equilibrium in the country's balance of payments[9].

"Fostering" certain conditions suggests an active rather than passive role, and "encouraging a more sustainable rate of economic growth" implies that it is the consensus that the present growth rate is not "sustainable" and must be retarded.

The vote on the directive was unanimous—a fact that should be considered a strengthening modifier of the directive. Dissenting votes imply that the chairman's position summarized in the directive is weak.

The section headed "Authority to Effect Transactions in System Account" is a detailed summary of economic reports, staff economic projections, Treasury activities, recent open market operations, etc. A careful reading of this section further clarifies the intent of the directive. (These are the data available for the period since December 1961.) The complete minutes provide amplification of the materials mentioned above in the sense that the entire proceedings – reports, discussion, disagreement – are reported. This is the reason for expressing greater confidence in the interpretation of the Committee's directives for the period from March 1951, through December 1961.

In the absence of the elaborate information provided in the minutes of the Committee's meetings it is, nevertheless, possible to distinguish not only between expansionary and contractile directives but also, in most cases, between stronger and weaker instructions. To illustrate the point a sequence of records from the *Federal Reserve Bulletin* reporting the "Authority to Effect Transactions in System Account" based on Committee meetings on October 29, 1968, November 26, 1968, the following December 17, and January 14, 1969, will be considered[10].

On October 8, 1968, it was the expressed policy of the Federal Open Market Committee "to foster financial conditions conducive to sustainable economic growth, continued resistance to inflationary pressures, and attainment of reasonable equilibrium in the country's balance of payments." To implement the policy open market operations were to be designed to maintain "about the prevailing conditions in money and short-term credit markets. . . ." Taken alone and out of context this directive seems to have little substantive content. It is clear that there were some inflationary pressures but there was no dramatic change in policy. In fact, the wording of the directive was identical to that in the instruction issued by the Committee on August 13, 1968. In August, however, the consensus was unanimous, whereas the October 8 vote was split, with Messrs. Hayes, Hickman, and Kimbrel dissenting.

The wording of that part of the directive quoted was again unchanged in the instructions issued by the Committee on October 29 and on November 26, but neither was unanimous. On October 29 Mr. Hayes dissented (with Messrs. Hickman and Kimbrel joining the majority), and on November 26 the dissenting minority grew to four: Messrs. Hayes, Hickman, Kimbrel, and

Morris. The four who voted against the action reiterated the reasons previously given by the minority. They advocated "seeking somewhat firmer money market conditions in an effort to slow the rate of bank credit growth," which in their view had been excessive for several months. From only the information considered to this point it is clear that the policy in effect at the time was one of monetary restraint, but that it was intended to be a very mild form of restraint.

In the general section of the report which precedes the official directive, it was observed on August 13, 1968, that the vigorous expansion in progress at that time would probably slow down considerably in the next few months due to the recently approved 10% tax surcharge. Inflation was still a major problem at that time, but the Committee members were apparently unanimously persuaded that the long-awaited move toward fiscal restraint would quickly take effect.

On October 8, 1968, it was reported to the Committee that "estimates of GNP in the third quarter had been revised upward since the preceding meeting . . . mainly because consumer expenditures had proved stronger than expected." (The reduction in personal disposable income associated with an increase in personal income taxes had not brought about a quick decline in consumption.) Further complicating the situation was a disproportionate increase in imports of merchandise in relation to the small increase in exports. Inflation was obviously still the major economic problem faced by the monetary policymakers; this fact was reflected by the three dissenting votes.

At the meeting held on October 29, despite continued strength of consumer spending and rising prices, a note of optimism was struck. It was reported that "expansion in real GNP moderated somewhat in the third quarter, according to preliminary Commerce Department estimates." With this news and other details of the economy's performance the minority dissenting declined to a single member, Mr. Hayes.

With the expansion "still strong" and Industrial Production (traditionally an excellent proxy for real GNP) increasing at an increasing rate, the minority again grew and at the November 26 meeting there were four dissenters. (Recall that the wording of the directive was unchanged from that of August 13, October 8, and October 29.)

On December 17, 1968, the "current rate of expansion in over-all economic activity was significantly higher than had been projected earlier. . . ." Inflation was not only the major problem; it was apparently getting worse. Sizable deficits in the balance of payments were developing. Retail sales were up, interest rates had risen sharply on securities of all maturities, and estimates of the growth rate of bank credit had been revised upward. Note the change in the wording of the directive:

> In this situation, it is the policy of the Federal Open Market Committee to foster financial conditions conducive to the reduction of inflationary pressures, with a view to encouraging a more sustainable rate of economic growth and attaining reasonable equilibrium in the country's balance of payments.
>
> To implement this policy, System open market operations until the next meeting of the committee shall be conducted with a view to attaining firmer conditions in money and short-term credit markets. . . .

This wording reflects an obvious shift in monetary policy—not from contractionary to expansionary but from a weak policy of restraint to a strong one. In evaluating the length of the lag in effect of monetary policy it is far more important to distinguish between weak and strong instructions than simply between periods when the policy is expansionary or contractionary. When the directive is weak it may be that other determinants of monetary fluctuations completely obscure the effects of discretionary policy actions. When the instruction is sufficiently strong to insure that open market operations will exert the primary, if not exclusive, influence on money and credit conditions, then the effects of policy decisions should be apparent despite the operation of unmanaged factors.

The Criteria for Assigning Values to Policy Decisions

In evaluating the policy decisions of the Federal Open Market Committee for purposes of applying nonparametric analysis to the data, an attempt has been made not only to differentiate between expansionary and contractile prescriptions but also to order each type of instruction by intensity. Very weak or neutral policy positions have been regarded as zero elements; progressively stronger expansionary instructions have been assigned values from one through four; progressively stronger restrictive monetary policy decisions, values from minus one through minus four.

No tremendous significance is claimed for the rank orderings—particularly for those covering the secondary period. This study in no way utilizes rank order significance tests, so the arbitrary division of strong negative and positive instructions into classes does not influence the probability estimates. The original purpose in drawing such distinctions was to lend some flexibility to the process of identifying the level at which an instruction became strong enough to produce an identifiable effect. The analysis reported in this study, however, uses only the originally identified zero elements as weak instruction, all positive or negative elements being treated as equally strong.

The criteria by which the rankings were assigned can be divided into seven broad categories (although the groupings were not specified before the evaluation was made). These categories can be described for convenience as: (a) formal, (b) participatory, (c) technical, (d) impressionistic, (e) dissentient, (f) provincial, and (g) incremental. The significance of the categories varies depending upon the particular report being evaluated. A brief discussion of these categories will help to clarify the considerations involved in assigning ranks to open market policy decisions.

The formal category involves an evaluation of the specific language of the directive on which the vote is taken. More important than the language of each directive are the subtle changes which occur from one instruction to the next as shifts in policy occur. Analysis of this particular factor should be done separately from most of the others so that long sequences of directives can be considered together.

The classification "participatory" designates the consideration of voting patterns. Often as the policy is about to change there will be an early indication of the trend by dissenting votes. Very little consideration was given to the identities and backgrounds of the voting members in the present study, but it may be that an investigation of this type would prove very fruitful indeed. Review of the participatory factor should be simultaneous with that of the formal one so that sequential developments may be observed.

Staff reports and economic forecasts have been classified as "technical." The Committee members certainly must rely heavily on these reports when attempting to formulate an effective monetary policy; therefore, the importance of the technical factor is very great. It is interesting to note, with respect to this category, that the content of the economic reports and forecasts—whether subsequent developments confirm or deny their accuracy—is the important consideration in evaluating the policy formulated at a given Committee meeting. This observation is based on the fact that subsequent developments and data revisions are unknown at the time when the policies are being implemented. In fact, one of the other aspects of the technical category is its potential usefulness to the manager of the trading desk at the Federal Reserve Bank of New York. In all probability his interpretation of the Committee's directive is colored by the content of these economic reports; hence, any subsequent evaluation of the policy established at a given meeting should be influenced by the reports and forecasts presented at that meeting.

The adjective "impressionistic" has been used to describe the brief summary of the important points discussed at the meeting. This summary is useful as an index to the details of the entire content of the minutes of a given meeting, but—even more important—it is a striking reflection of the chairman's judgment of the relative significance of the matters which were discussed at the meeting.

Many Committee meetings can be characterized as debates in which individuals disagree about economic conditions, remedies, and degrees of intensity of monetary policy. This aspect of the record has been labeled "dissentient." It is a separate category from "participatory" because, first, there is often apparent reconciliation of positions, hence unanimity on the final policy decision, and, second, the details of the debate may influence the actions of the manager of the trading desk to some extent.

The modifier "provincial" is not used in a pejorative sense but as a term which implies that some of the reports and discussions at the meetings of the Committee reflect the interests of groups in specific geographical areas. The attendance and participation of Federal Reserve Bank presidents–even those not serving on the Committee at the time–is apparently encouraged. This provides a kind of economic representation which doubtless influences policy as well as the interpretation (and execution) of the orders issued. If so, then any attempt to interpret the policy decisions would be incomplete without some considerations having been given to the "provincial" factor.

Finally, quite significant influences on the strength and speed of the effects of monetary policy are the augmenting policy actions taken by the Federal Reserve Board. These actions have been categorized as "incremental" because of their potential for intensifying the effects of Federal Open Market Committee decisions. For example, if the reserve requirement should be increased during a period in which the prevailing directive for open market operations is one of monetary restraint, it would be expected that the effects of monetary restraint would occur earlier and show greater intensity. Other such policy-augmenting actions are discount rate changes, adjustments to the ceilings on time deposit interest rates which commercial banks may pay, changes in stock market trading margin requirements, and so on.

As mentioned above, this list of categories was compiled only after the ranking of policy decisions had been made. The information recorded in the minutes of the meetings of the Federal Open Market Committee suggested the classifications–not the reverse. These somewhat arbitrary divisions are useful as a catalog of the kinds of considerations which influenced the assignment of ranks for the present study. They may also have some value as a guide to interpreting additional open market minutes.

The Appendix is a listing by date of all official Federal Open Market Committee meetings held from January 1951, through January 1970. Rankings for the first decade (through December 1961) are based on the extensive information provided by the complete record in the minutes. Data for the most recent period were found in the *Annual Reports* of the Board of Governors of the Federal Reserve System and, since January 1967, in the monthly issues of the *Federal Reserve Bulletin.* The interpretations of policy directives for the earlier period are naturally somewhat more reliable than those for the most recent years. Classifications for the last 8 years are: active expansion, active restraint, and passive.

Chapter 5 is an explanation of the theoretical framework underlying the empirical study to be reported in Chap. 6. The theoretical section is not intended to be a specification of a set of structural relationships to be estimated and tested but a rationale for assuming that monetary policy decisions influence some economic aggregates after a lag. In accordance with the stated purpose of this study, the theoretical construct to be evaluated is simply an hypothesized relationship between the decisions of a policy-making body and subsequent macroeconomic developments reflected in various aggregate economic series.

Notes

1. Letter from William McChesney Martin, Jr. to Dr. Wayne C. Grover published in *Federal Reserve Bulletin,* vol. 50 (August 1964), p. 1015.
2. *Ibid.,* p. 1016.
3. *Ibid.*
4. *Federal Reserve Bulletin,* vol. 53 (July 1967), pp. 1168-1169.
5. *Ibid.,* p. 1115.

6. Elmus R. Wicker, *Federal Reserve Monetary Policy 1917-1933* (New York: Random House, 1966), p. ix.

7. *Federal Reserve Bulletin,* vol. 50 (February 1964), 154; ("Statement on Proposed Changes in Federal Reserve Act" by William McChesney Martin, Jr., Chairman, Board of Governors of the Federal Reserve System, before the Subcommittee on Domestic Finance of the House Committee on Banking and Currency, Jan. 2, 1964).

8. *Federal Reserve Bulletin,* vol. 55 (June 1969), p. 514.

9. *Ibid.*

10. Quotations in the discussion which follows are from the *Federal Reserve Bulletin,* vols. 54 and 55 (November 1968, through May 1969.)

5

A Theoretical Framework for Monetary Policy Lag Analysis

Exogenous and Endogenous Variables: The Debate between the Keynesians and the Neoclassicists

The attempt to measure the lag in effect of monetary policy implicitly assumes that monetary variables exert an important influence on the economy. This assumption is well established in economic theory; few economists would deny that "money matters." There is considerable disagreement, however, concerning the issues of how much influence monetary variables exert and through what mechanism the effects are realized. The arguments pro and con are usually presented in theoretical terms, but the basic disagreement appears to be empirical rather than theoretical[1].

It is not the purpose of this book to evaluate the merits of the various monetarist systems versus those of the post-Keynesian income-expenditure schemes. Regardless of the theoretical framework chosen, the fact that fluctuations in monetary variables do influence the level of economic activity (in the short run at least) seems inescapable. Extreme advocates of the quantity theory approach tend to relegate the effects of monetary policy exclusively to nonreal variables. For example, the Cambridge quantity version presents the equation of exchange in a form that implies a constant velocity of money:

$$M = kPQ \qquad (5\text{-}1)$$

(where M is the quantity of money, P is the price level, Q is real output, and k is the reciprocal of constant velocity). This equation is useful for analysis in some contexts, but it removes the "account-balancing" function from velocity and, assuming instantaneous adjustment, implies that changes in the supply of money are reflected in price increases, output being determined independently.

At the other extreme, some proponents of an exclusive income-expenditures approach assume that the price level is given in the short run, its determinants being institutional factors which operate outside the system of economic variables. The determination of the equilibrium level of real output and the interest rate are regarded purely as a matter of equating saving and investment. The money supply, in this extreme view, is taken as an endogenously determined variable.

A Three-Sector Macroeconomic Model

Actually, as suggested by Friedman[2], most economists could agree on a theoretical model incorporating such variables as real income, interest rates, prices, employment, and real wages. Their disagreement would arise from their different assumptions about which variables are determined within the system and which are exogenous. As a basis for a discussion of the explanation of the income-adjustment lag, a simple model will be presented[3].

First, the national income accounting identity,

$$\frac{Y}{P} = \frac{C + I}{P} \tag{5-2}$$

states that real income, i.e., nominal income Y divided by the price level P, is equal to consumption C plus investment I both divided by price. (The price level could be factored out of the equation entirely, but it is useful as a reminder that there is a difference between nominal and real quantities.) The identity holds because income is identically equal to output and because that output which is produced in the current accounting period but is not consumed in the same period is defined as investment. Businessmen may purchase goods in order to build up their inventories; these purchases are considered investment. If sales should fall below the level forecasted and, as a result, the same businessmen should accumulate inventory unintentionally, this increase in inventory is again placed in the investment category. Because it is unintended investment, however, the effect is different: new orders are reduced, suppliers curtail production, unemployment rises, and income falls. (Government taxes and expenditures have been omitted from the analysis for simplicity; however, incorporating these variables would not change the conclusions of this particular analysis.)

So far it has simply been assumed that sales either do or do not materialize as expected without any discussion of the causes of discrepancies. Although the factors influencing the levels of consumption and investment are many and complex, they can be expressed in the following highly abstract forms:

$$\frac{C}{P} = c\left(\frac{Y}{P}, r\right) \tag{5-3}$$

$$\frac{I}{P} = i\,(r) \tag{5-4}$$

Equation (5-3) states that consumption C in real terms (discounted for variations in the price level) is a function c of real income and the interest rate r. It is important to recall that the model is static and all factors are in perfect balance or stable equilibrium. No allowance has been made for disequilibria or adjustments over time.

The real value of consumption has been assumed to be systematically related to real income and the interest rate. The form of the function has not been specified but it has been assumed that

$$\frac{\partial c}{\partial (Y/P)} > 0 \quad \text{and} \quad \frac{\partial c}{\partial r} < 0$$

It it intuitively obvious that consumption will tend to increase as income increases, *ceteris paribus.* The relationship of consumption to variations in the interest rate is not so clear. The rationale for including the rate of interest as an argument in the consumption function is that increased saving (reduced consumption) can be induced by increasing the reward (interest rate) for saving. This consideration is probably more important during periods of full employment when increases in investment may bid up the yield on bonds due to the lack of idle investment capital.

Equation (5-4) expresses the assumption that investment I is some function i of the rate of interest r. It is intended that the symbol r will serve not only as an index of the level of interest rates generally but also as an indicator of the availability of funds. It is assumed that $\partial i/\partial r < 0$; i.e., when interest rates fall (and funds become more readily available), investment will increase and conversely.

Equations (5-2), (5-3), and (5-4) constitute what is generally referred to as the expenditure sector of the model. Substituting (5-3) and (5-4) into (5-2) and solving for Y/P produces the algebraic equivalent of the familiar IS curve. It is a statement of the range of possible combinations of real income and interest rates at which the demand for and supply of real goods would be equal.

The monetary factors of the economy can be summarized in three equations:

$$\frac{M^d}{P} = 1\left(\frac{Y}{P}, r\right) \quad (5\text{-}5)$$

$$M^s = h\,(F, u) \quad (5\text{-}6)$$

$$M^d = M^s \quad (5\text{-}7)$$

Equation (5-5) states that the demand for real cash balances, i.e., the demand for nominal balances M^d discounted for the price level, is a function 1 of real income and the interest rate. The partial derivatives are:

$$\frac{\partial M^d}{\partial\,(Y/P)} > 0 \quad \text{and} \quad \frac{\partial M^d}{\partial r} < 0$$

(Note that the demand for money is determined both by income and the interest rate regardless of the interest elasticity of the transactions demand for cash.)

The money supply function in (5-6) is an attempt to reflect the influence of both Federal Reserve policy F and various unmanaged factors u on the supply of money M^s. The assumption of instantaneous adjustment implied by the static model suggests that the stock of money is controlled by F only, the expected value of u being zero. The equilibrium assumption in (5-7) means that the right-hand sides of (5-5) and (5-6) can be equated and, in turn, a solution for values of Y/P consistent with values of r obtained. This solution is equivalent to the LM curve.

Two systems of equations, representing the real goods sector and the monetary sector, have been produced, both expressing Y/P in terms of r. In combination, these equations determine the level of income and the interest rate for a given price level (neglecting the influence of government and foreign trade). Vary the price level and the income–interest rate coordinates vary. In effect, the solution is an aggregate demand equation which specifies not only the quantities which will be purchased at all possible prices but also the levels of the rate of interest with which the demand coordinates are consistent. A determinate solution which includes the equilibrium price level must involve a supply equation which would specify the quantities of output for all possible price levels. The equation required must incorporate the determinants of output.

On the assumptions that the capital stock is fixed in the short run and that labor is the only relevant short run variable, the following relationships are postulated:

$$\frac{Y}{P} = f(N) \tag{5-8}$$

$$\frac{W}{P} = f'(N) \tag{5-9}$$

$$N = j\left(\frac{W}{P}\right) \tag{5-10}$$

Equation (5-8) states that real income (output) is some function f of the level of employment N. As the number of production employees increases, the total output increases (although at a decreasing rate), i.e.,

$$\frac{\partial f}{\partial N} > 0 \quad \text{and} \quad \frac{\partial^2 f}{\partial N^2} < 0$$

Equation (5-9) is a statement of the assumption that entrepreneurs attempt to maximize profits; they will add employees to the work force up to that point at which the value of the increment to production is just equal to the increase in cost, which, in this case is the real wage, i.e., nominal wages W discounted for the price level. The labor supply equation is (5-10) which states, assuming

$$\frac{\partial j}{\partial (W/P)} > 0$$

that the higher the real wage the larger the number of workers who will be willing to work (or the more hours per period the workers will be willing to work).

If the nominal wage is given, then Eqs. (5-8) and (5-9) combine to produce an aggregate supply function which specifies the quantities of output which will be produced at all possible prices. The combination of this supply function with the aggregate demand function identifies an equilibrium level of price and output as well as the levels of employment, real wage, and interest rates which are consistent with that equilibrium (for a given money wage).

A Reduced Form of the Model and an Analysis of Expected Elasticities with Respect to the Money Stock

Smith[4] and others have summarized similar models as three simultaneous equations of the form:

$$y = c(y, r) + i(r) \tag{5-11}$$

$$\frac{M}{P} = l(y, r) \tag{5-12}$$

$$\frac{W}{P} = f'(N) \tag{5-13}$$

where $y = Y/P$, $c = C/P$, $i = I/P$, and $f'(N)$ is the marginal productivity of labor. In this form the model can be utilized to evaluate the combined effects of policy actions on various target variables, bearing in mind, of course, that the validity of any conclusions depends upon the consistency of the underlying assumptions with reality. For example, it has been assumed that institutional constraints determine the equilibrium income velocity of money within a narrow range; and, therefore, if a given level of real income is to be maintained, wage and price increases must be monetized by the central bank, i.e., W and P are implicit functions of M.

The major disagreement between economists of the two schools mentioned above arises from the empirical issue concerning the identification of endogenous and exogenous variables. Are prices and wages institutionally determined variables which are essentially fixed in the short run? Is real income a "given" which cannot be influenced by factors operating through the monetary and income-expenditures sector? These are empirical questions, of course, but theoretical analysis may identify the variables which should be measured in order to formulate answers. To illustrate this point the model which has been presented will be used in its three-equation summarized form to analyze the theoretical effects of changes in the stock of money on the level of prices, interest rates, and output.

First, Eqs. (5-11) through (5-13) are differentiated partially with respect to M producing

$$\frac{\partial y}{\partial M} = \frac{\partial c}{\partial y}\frac{\partial y}{\partial M} + \frac{\partial c}{\partial r}\frac{\partial r}{\partial M} + \frac{\partial i}{\partial r}\frac{\partial r}{\partial M} \tag{5-14}$$

$$\frac{1}{P} - \frac{M}{P^2}\frac{\partial P}{\partial M} = \frac{\partial 1}{\partial y}\frac{\partial y}{\partial M} + \frac{\partial 1}{\partial r}\frac{\partial r}{\partial M} \tag{5-15}$$

$$\frac{1}{P}\frac{\partial W}{\partial M} - \frac{W}{P^2}\frac{\partial P}{\partial M} = \frac{\partial\,[f'(N)]}{\partial M} \tag{5-16}$$

Solving for dP/dM yields

$$\frac{dP}{dM} = \frac{P}{M}\left[\frac{M}{W}\frac{\partial W}{\partial M} - \frac{M}{f'(N)}\frac{\partial\,[f'(N)]}{\partial M}\right]$$

which can be written

$$\frac{M}{P}\frac{dP}{dM} = \frac{M}{W}\frac{\partial W}{\partial M} - \frac{M}{f'(N)}\frac{\partial\,[f'(N)]}{\partial M} \tag{5-17}$$

This result states, simply, that the elasticity of prices with respect to changes in the money stock is exactly equal to the elasticity of nominal wages with respect to changes in the money stock less the elasticity of the marginal physical productivity of labor with respect to changes in the money stock. If a 10% increase in the money supply is accompanied by a 10% increase in wages, then prices too must rise by 10% unless there is an increase in the marginal productivity of labor. If a 10% increase in the money stock produces no change in the nominal wage or in the marginal physical productivity of labor, then prices will remain stable and, it follows from the model, real income will rise.

The converse also holds and, from a policy viewpoint, is perhaps more important. If wages rise by 10% in the absence of any increase in real output, then the money stock must be increased in order to allow prices to rise by an equivalent percentage or output will fall until the real wage is again equal to the marginal productivity of labor. This means that inflation cannot persist in the absence of monetary expansion within the framework of the model.

Simultaneous solution of Eqs. (5-14), (5-15), and (5-16) for the total change in interest rates with respect to a change in the money stock and conversion of the result into an elasticity expression produces the following:

$$\frac{M}{r}\frac{dr}{dM} = \frac{M}{P}\,\frac{\left[1 - \frac{\partial c}{\partial y}\right]\left[1 - \frac{M}{W}\frac{\partial W}{\partial M} + \frac{M}{f'(N)}\frac{\partial\,[f'(N)]}{\partial M}\right]}{r\left[\frac{\partial l}{\partial r}\left(1 - \frac{\partial c}{\partial y}\right) + \frac{\partial l}{\partial y}\left(\frac{\partial c}{\partial r} + \frac{\partial i}{\partial r}\right)\right]} \qquad (5\text{-}18)$$

The term on the left is, of course, the elasticity of the interest rate with respect to a change in the money stock. On the right M/P is nominal balances discounted for the prevailing price level, i.e., real balances. The entire denominator of the complex fraction is assumed to be negative for the following reasons. $\partial c/\partial y$ is the change in consumption as real income changes, therefore, a positive fraction which implies that the quantity $(1 - \partial c/\partial y)$ is also a positive fraction. $\partial l/\partial r$ is negative since this is the measure of the change in the demand for money with respect to changes in the rate of interest. The product of the two expressions must, then, be negative. Similarly the product of $\partial l/\partial y$ (the change in the demand for money as income changes, which is positive) and $(\partial c/\partial r + \partial i/\partial r)$ (the changes in consumption and investment with respect to interest rate changes, which are negative) must be negative. The sum of the two negative values multiplied by the (positive) interest rate r produces a negative denominator.

In the numerator, the expression on the left hand side is clearly positive as explained above. This means that the crucial factors in determining the elasticity of the rate of interest with respect to changes in the money supply are $(M/W)\ (\partial W/\partial M)$, the elasticity of wages with respect to the money stock, and $[M/f'(N)]\ \{\partial[f'(N)]/\partial M\}$, the elasticity of the marginal physical productivity of labor with respect to changes in the money supply. If the elasticity of wages less the elasticity of marginal physical productivity, both with respect to changes in the money stock, are equal to unity, then changes in the money stock would have no effect on the interest rate (in the context of the model). If the difference between these elasticities were less than unity, the elasticity of interest rates with respect to the money supply wc ·ld be negative as expected.

A most interesting result would be obtained if subtracting the elasticity of marginal physical productivity with respect to changes in the stock of money from that of nominal wages should produce a difference greater than unity. This changes the sign of the numerator from positive to negative and implies a positive elasticity of interest rates with respect to the money stock!

It has been shown that, under the present assumptions, the effects of changes in the money stock on both interest rates and prices is significantly influenced by the elasticity of wages and productivity with respect to the money stock. Intuitively, then, it would seem that the efficacy of monetary policy as a tool for influencing real income may depend largely upon the elasticity of wages with respect to the money supply. This proposition can be checked in the context of the model by solving Eqs. (5-14), (5-15), and (5-16) simultaneously for dy/dM, the change in real income with respect to a change in the money supply. The result, expressed again as an elasticity is:

$$\frac{M}{y}\frac{dy}{dM} = \frac{1}{V} \frac{\left[\frac{\partial c}{\partial r} + \frac{\partial i}{\partial r}\right]\left[1 - \frac{M}{W}\frac{\partial W}{\partial M} + \frac{M}{f'(N)}\frac{\partial [f'(N)]}{\partial M}\right]}{\frac{\partial 1}{\partial r}\left[1 - \frac{\partial c}{\partial y}\right] + \frac{\partial 1}{\partial y}\left[\frac{\partial c}{\partial r} + \frac{\partial i}{\partial r}\right]} \qquad (5\text{-}19)$$

Equation (5-19) states that the elasticity of real income with respect to changes in the money stock is equal to the product of the reciprocal of income velocity V and the complex expression on the right. The denominator as well as the left hand term in the numerator of the complex fraction are all negative as explained above so that if

$$\left[\frac{M}{W}\frac{\partial W}{\partial M} - \frac{M}{f'(N)}\frac{\partial [f'(N)]}{\partial M}\right] \begin{cases} < 1, & \text{then } e_{yM} > 0 \\ = 1, & \text{then } e_{yM} = 0 \\ > 1, & \text{then } e_{yM} < 0 \end{cases}$$

If the difference between the elasticities of nominal wages and the marginal physical productivity of labor (both with respect to changes in the money stock) is less than unity, then the elasticity of real income with respect to changes in the money stock will be positive, etc.

There is implicit in the analysis an assumption that velocity is constant. When the assumption of instantaneous adjustment is dropped, the more realistic proposition that wealth holders attempt to maintain some stable relationship between real cash balances and real income replaces the assumption of constant velocity. If, for example, a wealth holder finds himself holding more in cash than he chooses he will attempt to reduce his level of cash balances by spending. But not all wealth holding units can reduce cash balances simultaneously, so the effect is that prices are bid up. At the same time, if the economy is not fully utilizing its resources, real output may also increase.

If all of the assumptions of the model were valid (including the assumption of perfect competition), the conclusions drawn would be correct. Many (perhaps most) of the assumptions are admittedly unrealistic; therefore the conclusions are necessarily subject to qualification. From the standpoint of statistical analysis—assuming that reliable data in the form of time series were available for all of the variables and that the statistical problems discussed in Chap. 3 could be obviated—any inferences would have to be qualified by a statement of the theoretical assumptions made. Estimates of coefficients and confidence limits would apply only under the most special conditions. Such are the problems encountered in the course of any econometric analysis.

Is the model, then, of no value? The answer, of course, depends upon its use. If subjecting a model to statistical tests is approached as a tentative attempt to identify certain economic relationships and patterns of adjustment, then the effort seems worthwhile. If a model is viewed as a mechanism by which the future may be predicted more or less accurately, the researcher will realize a measure of success only sporadically if at all. The likelihood of measuring the magnitudes of all of the relevant economic parameters as well as the distribution of the various time lags for a macroeconomic model seems remote. A more rewarding pursuit may be the less ambitious goal of identifying the signs of the derivatives and the probabilities that the expected signs will occur after a given time lapse. Such is the purpose of this study.

In the model presented, it was assumed that equilibrium real income was functionally related to the money supply (among other things).

$$\left(\frac{Y}{P}\right)^e = y^e = \phi\,(M) \tag{5-20}$$

Changes in the quantity of money supplied to the economy influence nominal income either through changes in real income or price changes or both.

The unrealistic assumption of instantaneous adjustment can be eliminated by writing current income as equal to income in the most recent period plus some constant proportion of the difference between equilibrium income and income in the most recent period:

$$y_t = y_{t-1} + \theta\,(y_t^{\,e} - y_{t-1}) \tag{5-21}$$

where $0 < \theta < 1$. If the adjustment coefficient θ is small, the adjustment lag from one equilibrium level to another will be long. If θ is large, the lag will be relatively short. (Instantaneous adjustment would mean that $\theta = 1$.)

Solving (5-21) for equilibrium income in time t yields

$$y_t^{\,e} = \frac{1}{\theta} y_t - \frac{1-\theta}{\theta} y_{t-1} \tag{5-22}$$

Next, the assumption that income in time t is influenced by the level of the money stock in, and only in, time t is exchanged for the assumption that income in time t is influenced by the level of the money stock in all previous periods:

$$y_t = a + \sum_{i=0}^{k-1} \beta_i M_{t-1} + \beta_k \sum_{j=0}^{\infty} \gamma^j M_{t-(k+j)} \tag{5-23}$$

where $0 < \gamma < 1$. The intercept term a allows for the possibility that in a linear regression the long-run elasticity of income with respect to the money stock may not be unity. The β coefficients for the current and last k−1 observed values for the money stock should be determined independently as indicated, on the assumption that the effects of monetary fluctuations on income may begin gradually, ascend to a peak, then subside. If the peak effect is to be correctly identified then k must be sufficiently large to insure that the maximum influence has occurred before the geometrically declining series specified by the second summation in (5-23) begins.

Obviously it would be impossible to include an infinite number of observations of M in a regression but the mathematical equivalent can be obtained by replacing the infinite sum with a simple function of y_{t-1} [5]. The proof of this substitution involves expressing the relationship described in (5-23) in terms of y_{t-1} and multiplying through by γ:

$$\gamma y_{t-1} = a\gamma + \sum_{i=0}^{k-1} \beta_i M_{t-(i+1)} + \beta_k \sum_{j=0}^{\infty} \gamma^{j+1} \times M_{t-(k+j+1)} \tag{5-24}$$

Subtracting (5-24) from (5-23) and rearranging produces

$$y_t = a(1-\gamma) + \beta_0 M_t + \sum_{i=1}^{k} (\beta_i - \gamma\beta_{i-1}) M_{t-1} + \gamma y_{t-1} \tag{5-25}$$

Combining (5-25) with (5-22) and simplifying yields the equilibrium level of real income expressed in terms of income in the past period and the level of the money stock in the current and past k periods:

$$y_t^e = \frac{a}{\theta}(1-\gamma) + \frac{1}{\theta}\beta_0 M_t + \frac{1}{\theta}\sum_{i=1}^{k} (\beta_i - \gamma\beta_{i-1}) M_{t-1} + \frac{1}{\theta}(\gamma + \theta - 1) y_{t-1} \tag{5-26}$$

The Rationale for Expecting Lags in Economic Effects

The purpose in adapting the model for lagged adjustment and expressing equilibrium income in the form of a linear regression equation was to present the rationale for the assumption (to be incorporated into the empirical work to follow) that the effects of changes in monetary policy may be distributed over several periods following the change[6]. In the usual regression analysis the goal is to estimate assumed structural parameters and to test their significance. This study, having established a theoretical rationale for the hypotheses to be tested, departs from the usual parametric approach.

Organization of the Data for a Nonparametric Analysis

It has been assumed that changes in monetary policy affect the level of nominal income subsequent to the time of the policy change. The null hypotheses to be tested involve a weak binomial assumption: if there is no correlation between monetary policy changes and subsequent changes in a particular target variable, then the probability that the direction of change in the policy variable will agree with that of the target variable in a given period approaches one-half as the number of observations increases without bound.

Let M designate an m-element vector of unit positive, or unit negative values representing policy decisions of the strong expansionary or strong contractile type as identified in Chap. 4. Let Y designate an n-element vector of unit positive or unit negative values representing expansion or contraction in some target variable (e.g., positive or negative first differences from the Federal Reserve's industrial production index). If the target vector is premultiplied by the transpose of the policy vector the result is an mXn matrix of unit positive and unit negative values. Positive values in the matrix indicate identical signs for the policy and target vector elements which produced the matrix element in question. Negative values result when the signs of the two elements which produced the product were opposite. Let the matrix produced by the premultiplication be designated A:

$$\mathbf{M}^{\mathrm{T}} \ \mathbf{X} \ \mathbf{Y} = \mathbf{A} \tag{5-27}$$

The null hypothesis based on the binomial assumption can be stated symbolically as

$$\frac{1}{n} \sum_{i=1}^{n} a_{ij} = 0 \tag{5-28}$$

where i = (1, 2, · · ·, n) and j = i, i = (1, 2, · · ·, n) and j = i+ 1, i = (1, 2, · · ·, n) and j = i + 2, · · ·, and finally i = (1, 2, · · ·, n) and j = i + k. If the relative frequency of agreement or disagreement of signs for any given lag period from zero to k months is significantly different from zero, then the null hypothesis (that there is no connection between changes in the policy variable and subsequent changes in the target variable) can be rejected. The kind of tests to which the empirical data will be subjected are an adaptation of this general form.

The analysis is not designed to evaluate the magnitude of the effects of policy decisions and, hence, will not reveal the "distribution" of the lag in the usual sense. It may, however, warrant the conclusion that, for the data involved, fluctuations in the target variable are systematically associated with earlier monetary policy decisions. Moreover, if the probabilities appear to increase, reach a peak, then decline over several periods, it can be concluded that the range of lag values for the data in question, defined by the first and last frequencies significantly different from those expected, identifies the approximate length of the lag distribution.

The average length of the lag in initial effect of monetary policy will be defined as the time period between the policy decision and the first significant effect observed. The average length of the lag in final effect of policy decisions will be identified by the last significant statistic. The time lag between policy directives and the cumulative magnitude in effect on the target variable cannot be identified by the nonparametric methods used.

A highly variable lag will reduce the frequency of successes in any given lag period, and, if the effect were distributed over a very short period, high variability might even eliminate all significant levels of success frequencies. If, on the other hand, succeeding periods of highly significant success ratios can be identified, this may be considered evidence in favor of a reliable lag.

Extrapolating from the study for the purpose of forecasting still implies the assumption that all of the structural parameters of the system are constant over time, an assumption which cannot be evaluated statistically. However, even the attempt at forecasting economic fluctuations from the conclusions produced by the nonparametric study is probably less risky than similar attempts based on parametric analysis because of the generality of the nonparametric technique. The results of a nonparametric analysis of the type proposed are presented and discussed in the next chapter.

Notes

1. Milton Friedman, "A Theoretical Framework for Monetary Analysis," *Journal of Political Economy,* vol. 78 (March/April 1970), p. 234.

2. *Ibid.,* p. 219.

3. The model is not original but to supply proper documentation would only shift the credit back one step in what, I suspect, would prove to be a lengthy chain. It is obviously quite similar to some of the models in Martin J. Bailey, *National Income and the Price Level,* (New York: McGraw-Hill, 1962).

4. Warren L. Smith, "A Graphic Exposition of the Complete Keynesian System," *Southern Economic Journal,* vol. 23 (October 1956), pp. 115-125.

5. Carl F. Christ, *Econometric Models and Methods* (New York: John Wiley and Sons, Inc., 1966), pp. 205-206.

6. The writer has used a logarithmic form of equation (5-26) to regress monthly observations of nominal personal income on current and 24 lagged values of the money stock (M_1 and M_2). The lagged income term assumed virtually all of the explanatory power for variations in current income; and when it was excluded

from the regression, the current level of the money stock plus the levels 12 and 24 months earlier were by far the most important. (Many of the coefficients of lagged values of the money stock were negative.) Coefficients of determination were naturally very high and standard errors of estimate were all relatively small, indicating that the trends of the two series were parallel.

The two most important conclusions of the analysis were (a) that the long-run elasticity of nominal income with respect to the money stock (M_1) is near unity and (b) that seasonal fluctuations in the money stock make current levels or those of 1, 2, or 3 years earlier better predictors of income than levels at, say, 3, 6, or 9 months before the predicted level of income.

6

Nonparametric Estimates of the Monetary Policy Lag for Selected Aggregate Indicators

The Meaning of Rejecting the Null Hypothesis

The last chapter was a theoretical justification of the assumptions basic to this study and a defense of the conclusion that there is a causal connection between monetary policy actions and the level of macroeconomic activity. Lagged values of the variables were incorporated into the function relating income to the monetary system in order to reflect the assumed dynamic nature of the adjustment process. The empirical estimates of the monetary policy adjustment lag reported in this chapter are based on the theoretical constructs of Chap. 5 only in the sense that the cause-effect relationships are a priori. No attempt has been made to estimate the model's structural parameters and no assumptions have been made with respect to the underlying distributions of the sampled populations. The nonparametric tests were designed to evaluate the null hypotheses that there are no systematic relationships between the observed fluctuations in the policy variable and those of the target variables. Rejection of a null hypothesis on basis of some assumed significance level is alleged to constitute proof neither of the theory nor of the assumed cause-effect relationships. Rejection of the null hypothesis is, first, a statement that the probability of the observed relationships' having occurred purely by chance is less than 5% (for an α value of 0.05). Second, it is the rationale for accepting the alternative hypothesis which states that there is some systematic association between the independent and dependent variables in question. Finally, rejecting the null hypothesis is justification for the statement that the sample values observed are not inconsistent with the theoretical relationships postulated.

The Form of the Statistical Tests

The nature of the statistical tests to which the data have been subjected was discussed in Chap. 5. Specific procedures employed in the actual manipulation of the data have been designed to obviate certain difficulties and to obtain a maximum of information from the data. For example, a review of the minutes of the meetings of the Federal Open Market Committee revealed that there were alternating periods in which monetary policy had swung from a strong macroeconomic stabilization program of the expansionary type to a relatively passive period or from a strong policy of monetary restraint back to a passive course again. The periods of restraint have been treated separately from those of expansionary policy on the assumption that the timing of the effects on the target variables may differ.

Periods in which the monetary policy could be considered passive have not been excluded from the analysis as the general discussion in Chap. 5 might imply. Instead, these periods have been considered "untreated" in the conventional contingency table context so that at least some of the influence of trends in the series has been eliminated. For example, suppose that the relative frequency of agreement in signs between the policy vector in periods of strong expansionary policy and certain lagged values of a given target variable were substantially greater than the 50% level. If the relative frequency of "untreated" positive first differences for the same lag period were equally high, then the correspondence in signs could be explained by the similar upward trends of the two series; hence, it would be misleading to reject the null hypothesis. Accordingly, the periods in which the monetary authorities have been passive from a macroeconomic stabilization standpoint have been included along with the periods characterized by strong policy instructions, the former being considered an untreated control group, the latter, a treated one.

The monthly data have been paired so that, in effect, the total number of successes and failures for all treated elements and all lag combinations from 0 to 24 months are known. (Recall that matching signs in corresponding elements of the policy and target vectors constitute successes.) These totals have been combined in two-by-two contingency tables with the data from the untreated periods so that a comparison of the number of subjects "living" and "dead" can be made between "treated" and "untreated" groups. Thus, for every different target vector there are 50 contingency tables by which the significance of the number of like corresponding signs for each of the present and 24 lagged values of the dependent variable may be tested both for expansionary monetary policy as well as for restraint.

Chi-square tests were applied to the sequence of two-by-two contingency tables representing each of the lag periods from 0 to 24 months. Two sets of 25 tests each were made for each of eight target variables in order to obtain a separate evaluation of the lags associated with expansionary and contractile policy. Four hundred separate chi-square tests, then, form the basis for the probability statements to be made. The chi-square statistics computed were of the form

$$\chi^2 = \frac{GT\,(|A_{11}A_{12} - A_{12}A_{21}| - \tfrac{1}{2}GT)^2}{(A_{11} + A_{12})\,(A_{21} + A_{22})\,(A_{11} + A_{21})\,(A_{12} + A_{22})} \qquad (6\text{-}1)$$

where $GT = \Sigma_{i=1}^{2} \Sigma_{j=1}^{2} A_{ij}$.

The data for the policy vector cover the 10-year period from January 1952, through December 1961, a sequence of 120 months involving four intervals of strong monetary restraint and three intervals of strong expansionary policy. The time span covered by the target vectors is the 12-year period from January 1952, through December 1963, the 24 additional observations supplying target vector values for the final 24 lag periods. Because the lag measure is implicitly discrete a significant incidence of successes for any given lag period is a reflection of the cumulative effects of previous policy actions. This cumulative effect tends to produce larger success frequencies after the initial effects accrue; hence, long periods of strong monetary policy directives may be expected to produce the highest chi-square values in later periods than very short intervals of strong monetary policy.

Definitions of the Policy and Target Vectors

The policy vector in each instance is the monthly sequence of prevailing instructions from the Federal Open Market Committee as interpreted by this writer on the basis of the minutes of the meetings of that Committee. Eight target vectors have been produced in the form of signs of first differences of time series. (The first difference sign in each case is entered in the position of the later month so that the lag estimates are again biased slightly upward.) The eight target variables were selected on the basis of the theoretical analysis of Chap. 5. In the process of solving for the elasticities of prices, interest rates, and real income with respect to changes in the money stock it developed that nominal wages were a crucial variable. The target variables selected, therefore, were meant to serve as surrogates for the four variables: prices, interest rates (including credit availability), real income, and the nominal wage. An additional target variable was selected as an indicator of the general level of economic activity, hence, a combination of the important macroeconomic factors of the American system.

Definitions of "Success" and "Failure"

The use of the signs of the first differences in the target variable series as indicators of success or failure is a stringent requirement. It is entirely conceivable that the effect of some policy actions on a given target variable may be simply to change the rate of change in the series without ever changing the sign of the first difference. If such an effect were consistent then it would represent a legitimate indicator for the measure of a lag in effect of monetary policy. Moreover, when the effect of policy actions is reflected in a change in the sign of the first derivative of the target variable, then the first effect of stabilization policy must have been to change the rate of expansion or contraction of the series. In other words, the lag in effect of monetary policy which this study is designed to measure is inherently longer than the lag from policy decision to the point at which the target variable begins to respond. The lag value for which the frequency of "successes" as defined becomes significant is a limit in the sense that the lag in first significant effect must necessarily be shorter. Because these comments as well as much of the analysis to follow apply to all of the target variables considered, the lag in effect of monetary policy on income will be discussed in detail first in order to simplify the subsequent treatment of the other target variables.

Analysis of the Lag in Effect on Income

The primary income proxy chosen was the monthly index of industrial production published in the *Federal Reserve Bulletin*. This series appears to have fluctuated approximately coincidentally with real income but with greater amplitude so that peaks and troughs are more readily detectable. The first differences of the series are biased toward positive values because of the secular trend but the analysis, as indicated above, was designed to adjust for the trend factor (although less effectively, perhaps, for the longest lag values). According to the theory presented in the previous chapter, industrial production, as a proxy for income, should have a positive derivative with respect to changes in the monetary variable except when the elasticity of nominal wages with respect to the monetary variable is equal to, or greater than, unity (adjusted for changes in the marginal physical productivity of labor).

On the assumption that economic adjustments are distributed over time, it was expected that the production index in the period in which the initial policy change occurred would reflect no significant reaction to the policy change. In some later period, assuming that monetary policy does influence income, the index of industrial production should begin to change in the same direction as the policy directive. If the time interval from policy decision to the observed effect were precisely the same each time, then at that particular lag value the frequency of successes would be 100% of the treated group. If, on the other hand, the effect should begin to be reflected by correct signs of the first difference earlier in some instances and later in others, then the relative frequency of successes for a given lag would be less than 100%. Even if the entire effect of a given monetary policy action were reflected in one, and only one, subsequent period in the target variable, any variation in the length of the lag would appear as diminished success probabilities distributed over several periods. Thus it may be that the successes measured in any given lag period are associated with several successive periods of strong policy decisions. Using historical data (instead of experimental data from the laboratory) requires, accordingly, that the average lag which is being measured be defined as the lag in effect of the average period of strong monetary policy instructions for the data in question. If, for example, in a given 10-year period there had been four distinct periods of strong monetary policy restraint the average length of which was 4½ months, then the estimated lag in effect of monetary restraint for that period would be associated with a 4- or 5-month interval of sustained monetary restraint.

During the 10-year period from January 1952, through December 1961, there were in fact four periods of strong monetary restraint averaging about 4½ months in duration. On the expansionary side there were three periods of strong policy directives averaging about 15 months each. (Identification of the periods of active and passive policy with respect to macroeconomic stabilization was made on the basis of the writer's interpretation of the minutes of the meetings of the Federal Open Market Committee as explained in Chap. 4.) The periods of expansionary policy were well separated so that there is little likelihood of overlapping effects between different expansionary sequences. This is not true of the periods of restraint. In fact, three of the four intervals of restraint occurred within a sequence of 17 months so that the entire period might be considered one of restraint. (The intervening weak instructions were mildly contractile.) Nevertheless, the statistical tests have been made purely on the basis of the original interpretation without regard to the possibility of overlapping effects.

Figures 6-1 and 6-2 show the values of chi square associated with the coincident and the first 20 months' lag in effect on industrial production for expansionary policy and restraint respectively. The symmetry in effect is interesting; the highest probabilities for occurrence of the expected signs in the first differences of the target variables appear in the seventh month after the initial strong policy directive for both the expanding and contracting series. From the preceding discussion it seems appropriate to conclude that the average lag in effect of monetary policy on real output (income) was 7 months or less for the period studied.

As indicated earlier, the arbitrarily selected alpha value for all significance tests in this study was 5%. This means that any lag period for which the data produced a chi-square value in excess of 3.841 reflects significant association between the policy and target variables at the 95% probability level. The test sequence for expansionary policy may be summarized as follows:

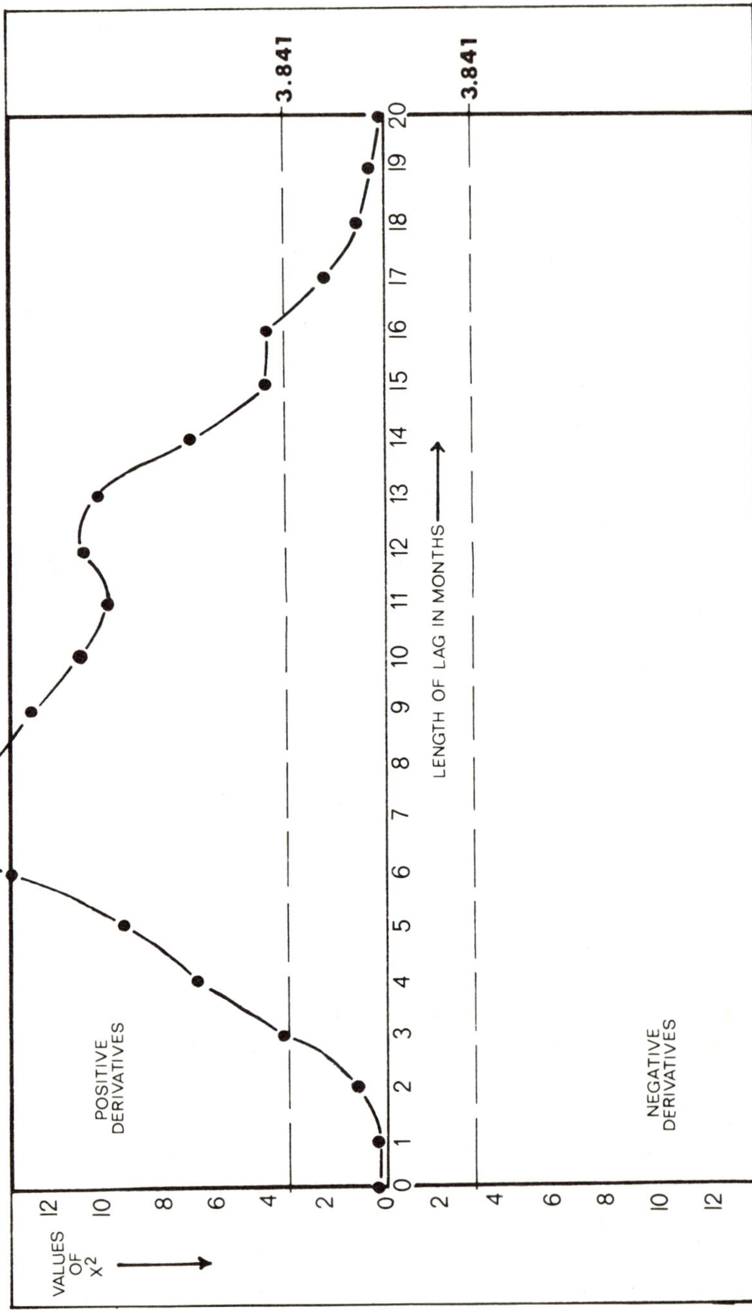

FIG. 6-1. Industrial production–monetary expansion.

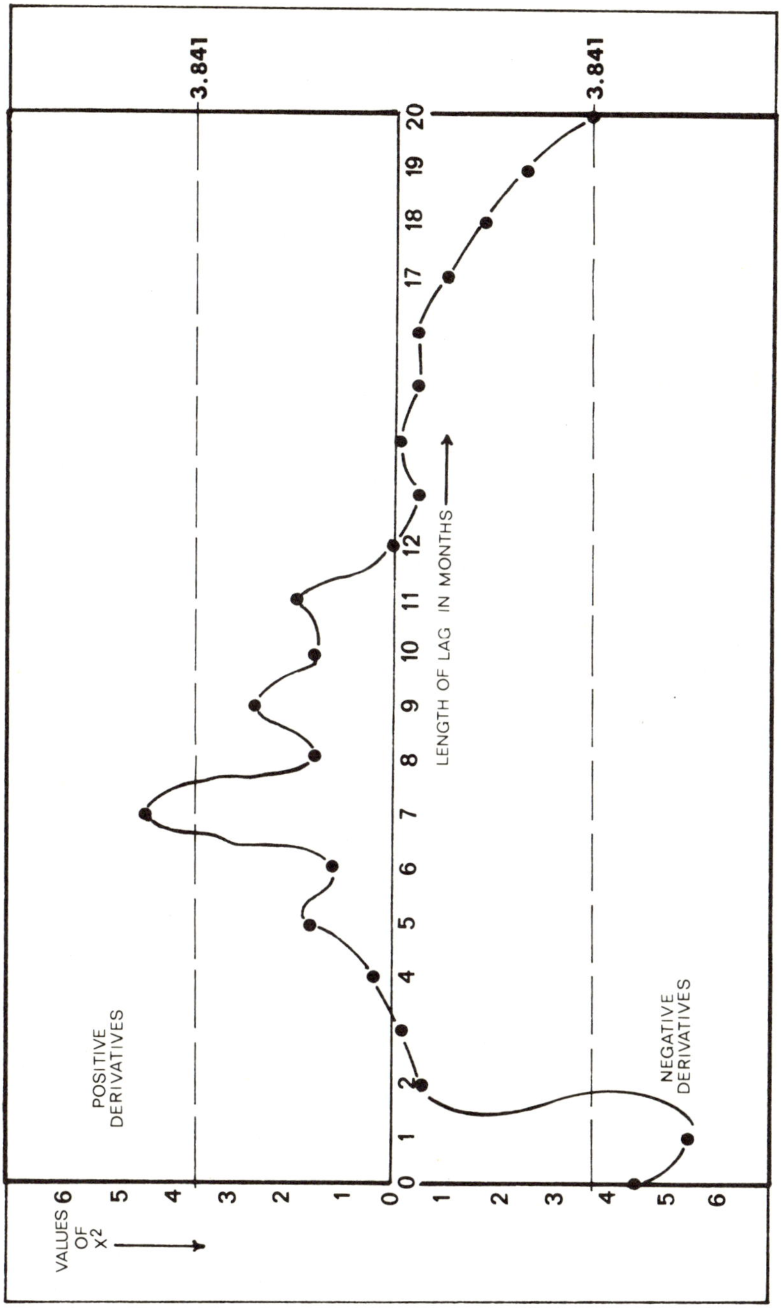

FIG. 6-2. Industrial production–monetary restraint.

1. H_0: The universe proportion of positive first differences in the index of industrial production series is independent of the corresponding signs of elements in the monetary policy vector for a lagged relationship of k periods.
2. H_A: The universe proportion is affected by the sign of monetary policy actions.
3. $a = 0.05$ (d.f.=1) requires a chi-square value of 3.841.
4. Criterion: Reject H_0 (and accept H_A) if $\chi^2 > 3.841$.
5. Compute χ^2 using formula (6-1) and apply criterion specified in step four.

The plotting of χ^2's in Fig. 6-1 indicates that, according to the established criterion, the null hypothesis must be rejected for all lag values from 4 through 16 months. Expansionary monetary policy directives do exert significant influence on the level of industrial production over the entire period beginning 4 months after the policy decision and continuing through the sixteenth month. The probability that any one of the success frequencies observed during that period could have occurred by chance is less than 5%.

Observe that the pattern of chi-square values reveals nothing at all concerning the magnitudes of the effects of monetary policy on industrial production. What is being measured is the reliability of the appearance of any significant effect at all after a given lag. The probability of occurrence of any discernible effect of monetary policy on the absolute level of production is highest after a 7-month lag for the data used in this study. The frequencies of successes observed between the fifth and fourteenth months were each of such relative magnitudes that the probability of their having occurred by chance was less than 1%. Two important observations should be made in this connection. First, the time period from policy action until industrial production begins to respond, i.e., begins to show a change in its rate of change, will always be shorter than the lag between a policy change and a corresponding change in the sign of the first difference of the production series.

Second, the 12-month period between the first significant chi-square value (at a 4-month lag) and the last significant statistic does not imply a highly variable lag. On the contrary, the fact that the corresponding signs of the policy and target vectors agree so frequently in each of the 12 periods that the occurrence cannot be attributed to chance is evidence of the fact that monetary policy effects occurred in those 12 lagged periods during the decade in question on a highly reliable basis. Here is strong evidence for the conclusion that the lag is distributed over several periods.

It has been mentioned that the average length of the three monetary expansion sequences during the decade in question was 15 months. Shorter periods of expansionary policy might have produced different lag patterns. However, the fact that the highest probability of success was associated with a 7-month lag suggests that the reinforcing effects of earlier policy actions began to decline abruptly after the seventh month. The reasoning behind this observation is based on the assumption that the number of successes observed for, say, the kth lag value reflects the cumulative effects from the first k periods of strong policy directives. If the number of significant successes observed in period k is less than that in period $k-1$, then apparently the reduction in the cumulative success frequency of the first k policy directives is greater than the increase in successes attributable to directive $k + 1$. From the foregoing reasoning it seems clear that policy effects produced by sustained sequences of strong instructions are apt to be equally reliable regardless of the length of the sequence, provided that it is not shorter than the period from the first strong directive to the peak in the chi-square series corresponding to the possible lag values. This means that the average length and variability of the lag in effect of monetary policy on the index of industrial production would have been approximately the same provided that the strong policy directives from the Federal Open Market Committee had persisted over a period of 7 months or more.

Although the peak probability for success occurs after a 7-month lag for both the expansionary and contractile policy series, the probabilities for success were consistently lower following retarding instructions during the decade in question. One aspect of the explanation for this observation is that the average length of the four monetary restraint sequences was only 4½ months;

therefore the frequency of successes observed in, say, the sixth lag period incorporated reinforcing effects from only 4 or 5 months of strong directives. That the lag value with the highest significance level is the same as that of the expansionary series indicates either (a) that the combined effects of 4 or 5 months of consistent strong policy occur with the greatest regularity after 7 months or (b) that the four periods of restraint should have been viewed as only two periods averaging about 11 months in duration.

A second aspect of the interpretation of the lower success probabilities associated with monetary restraint involves the decision-making process itself. The Federal Open Market Committee formulated its monetary policies with respect to macroeconomic stabilization during the 1950s and early 1960s on the basis of many important considerations–some explicit, some implicit (cf., Chap. 4). Some of the most important influences in the decision-making process were the economic reports presented by staff members to the Committee. These reports generally included estimates of the level of the index of industrial production. The monthly production index was obviously not the only variable considered but it appears to have been a fairly important indicator of the need for monetary restraint. This fact is demonstrated by the high chi-square values corresponding to the coincident and following months' "failure" frequencies for a policy of restraint. The negative derivative for industrial production with respect to the monetary variable indicates, simply, that the production series was being used as an indicator of the need for monetary restraint.

On the basis of the conclusion that the policy effects on production tend to diminish rapidly after the seventh month, the gradual development of significant negative derivatives after 19 or 20 months is not surprising. If a period of effective restraint were followed within 12 to 18 months by strong monetary expansion (as was the case in the 1950s), then the measure of "successes" and "failures" for monetary restraint, after 20 months, would naturally reflect a strong negative bias due to the efficacy of the expansionary policy.

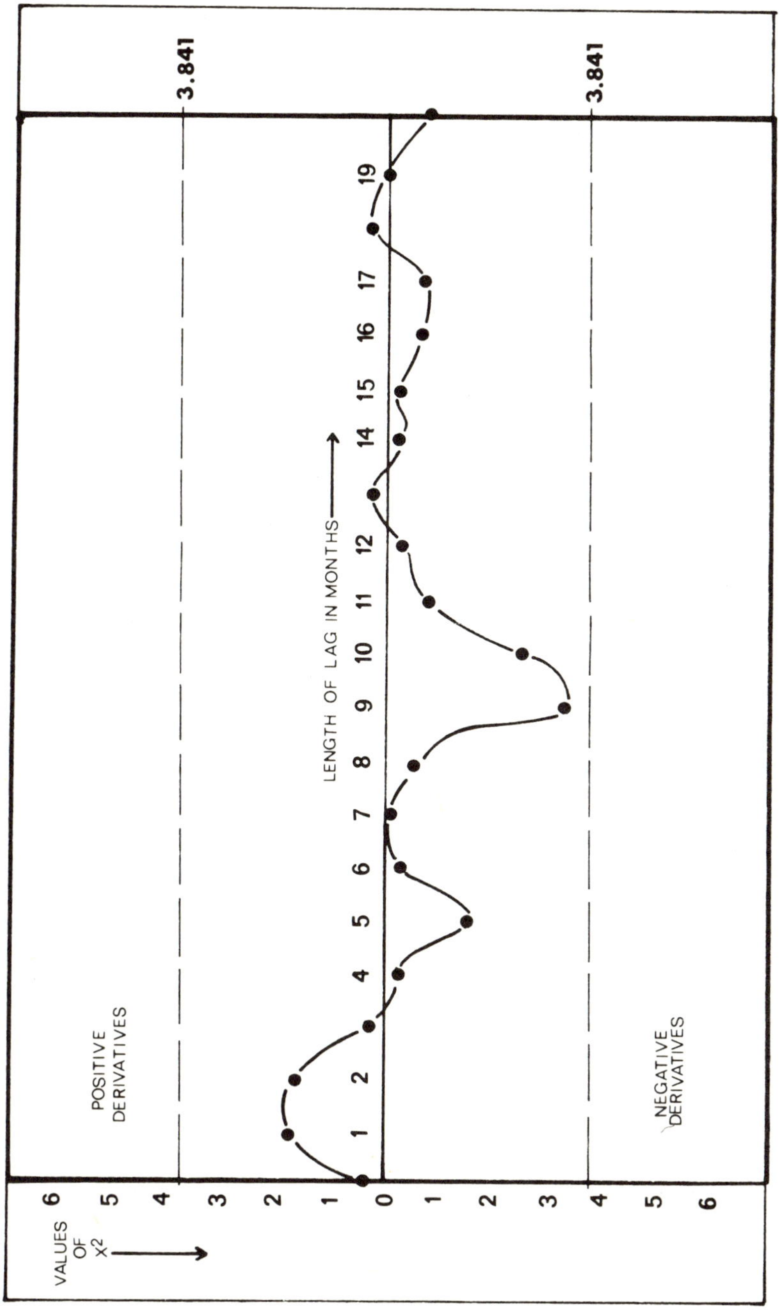

FIG. 6-3. Unemployment–monetary expansion.

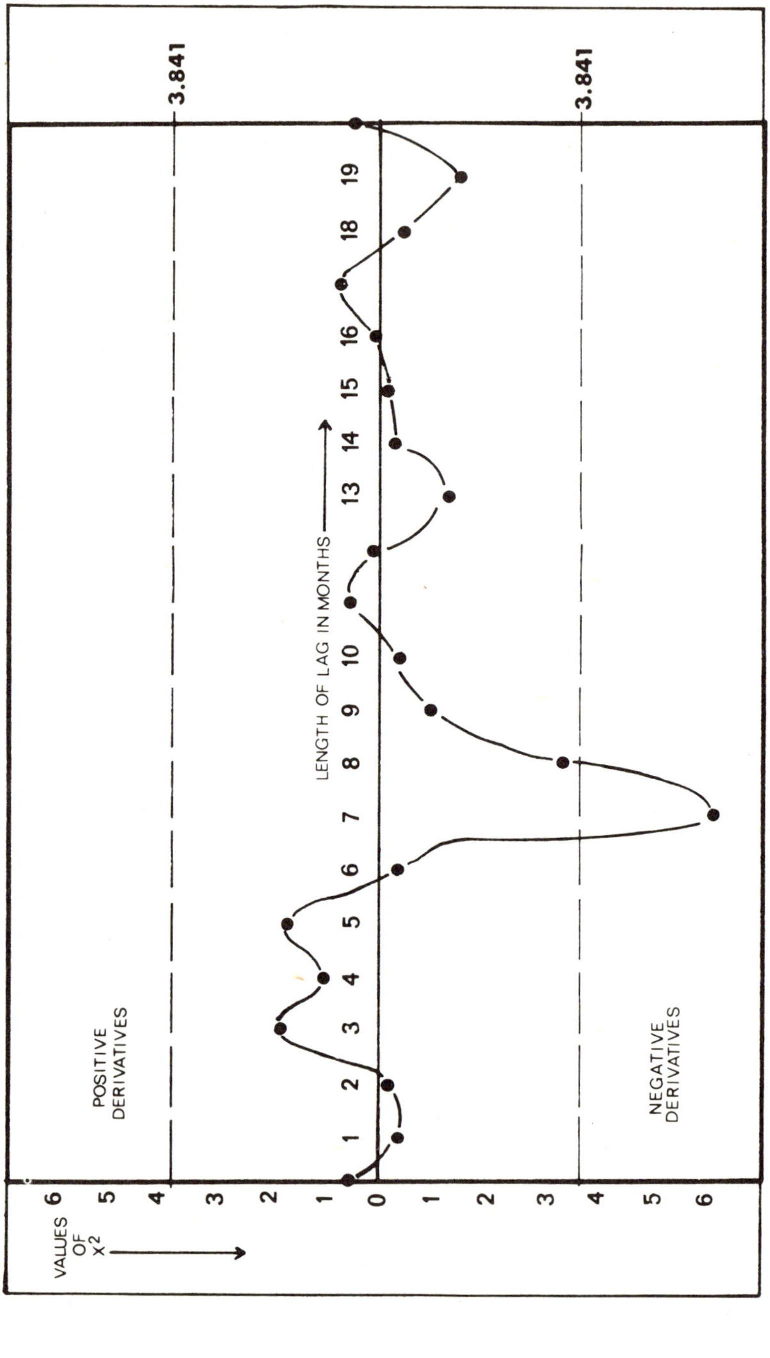

FIG. 6-4. Unemployment—monetary restraint.

A second indicator used to evaluate the effects of monetary policy on income was the level of unemployment. According to the theory presented in Chap. 5, real output (real income) is a function of the level of employment. By inference the level of unemployment is one measure of the degree to which the labor force is or is not being utilized productively. Unemployment is a particularly significant indicator in the American economy because a major part of the income distribution for the system is accomplished through the payment of wages. The target vectors in this case were constructed from the first differences in the monthly series of the number of unemployed in the civilian labor force as reported in the *Federal Reserve Bulletin.*

Under the assumptions of the theory presented, unemployment should fall as real output rises and conversely. The derivative of unemployment with respect to the monetary variable, then, should be negative. Figures 6-3 and 6-4 show the values of chi square associated with the coincident and first 20 months' lags in effect on unemployment for expansionary policy and restraint respectively. Only the seventh month after monetary restraint shows a significant frequency of successes (negative derivative) at the established criterion of $a = 0.05$. This observation is, of course, entirely consistent with the lag estimates for industrial production within the framework of the model. Monetary restraint produced a significant number of reductions in industrial production and increases in unemployment after only a 7-month lag.

The expansionary policy did not produce a significant observable reduction in unemployment (at the 5% alpha level) as the theory would predict, yet there were significant effects on the industrial production series. Does this phenomenon indicate an inconsistency in the theory? Recall that the unemployment series being used does not reflect variations in the average number of hours worked per week; thus output could easily rise on the basis of an increased average work week without any reduction in unemployment. The theory presented incorporated an assumption concerning the production sector to the effect that the derivative of the labor supply with respect to the real wage was positive.

If overtime pay is assumed to represent an increase in real wages, *ceteris paribus,* then the increase in labor input could be partly or entirely an increase in the average work week. This would seem normal for an economy operating at or near full employment.

It should be noted, incidentally, that there was a perceptible increase in the pattern of frequencies of observed "failures" (negative signs of first differences) in the eighth, ninth, tenth, and eleventh months after an expansionary monetary directive. In fact, the frequency observed after a 9-month lag was significant at an alpha level of 0.10. In other words, the probability that the observed number of signs discrepancies between the corresponding elements of the policy and target vectors could have occurred purely by chance is less than 10% for a 9-month lag. It appears, accordingly, that at least some of the effects of expansionary policy emerged in the form of reductions in unemployment.

A third important surrogate used for the income series was the composite estimate of aggregate economic activity published by the Department of Commerce in its *Business Conditions Digest.* This composite index is a weighted average of five aggregate economic series which are considered "coinciders" by the Department of Commerce statisticians. The specific series involved are (a) the number of employees on nonagricultural payrolls, (b) the total unemployment rate, (c) the index of industrial production, (d) personal income, and (e) manufacturing and trade sales.

In Figs. 6-5 and 6-6 are plotted the chi-square values for the current and first 20 lag periods associated with agreement between the signs of the policy and target variables. The effects of expansionary policy are reflected in Fig. 6-5; contractile, in Fig. 6-6. As in each instance in this study the elements of the target vectors are first differences.

It is interesting to note, first, that there is consistent disagreement in signs between the policy and target variables for a zero lag value. In the expansionary case the chi-square value indicates that the frequency of disagreement in signs is significant at the 2% probability level. The obvious interpretation of this

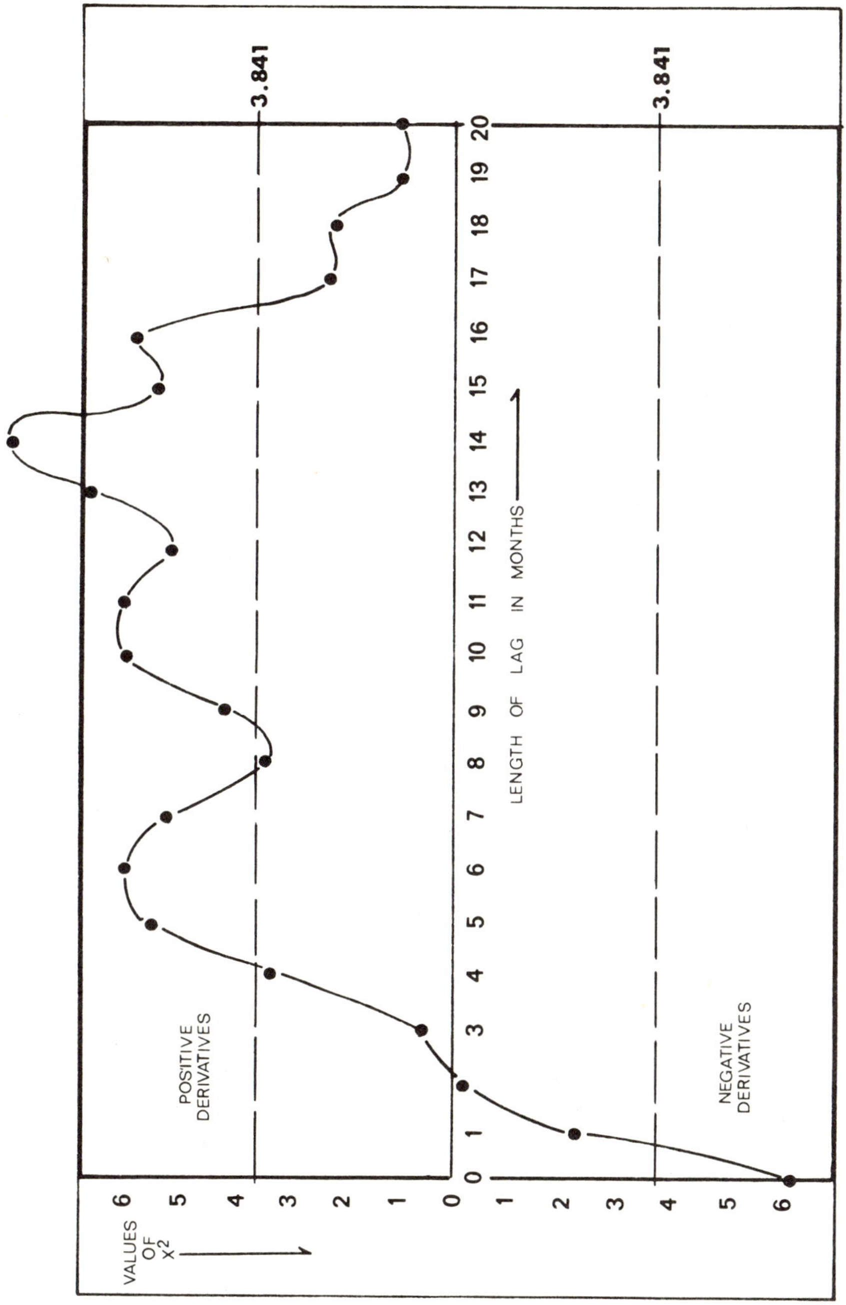

FIG. 6-5. Composite series—monetary expansion.

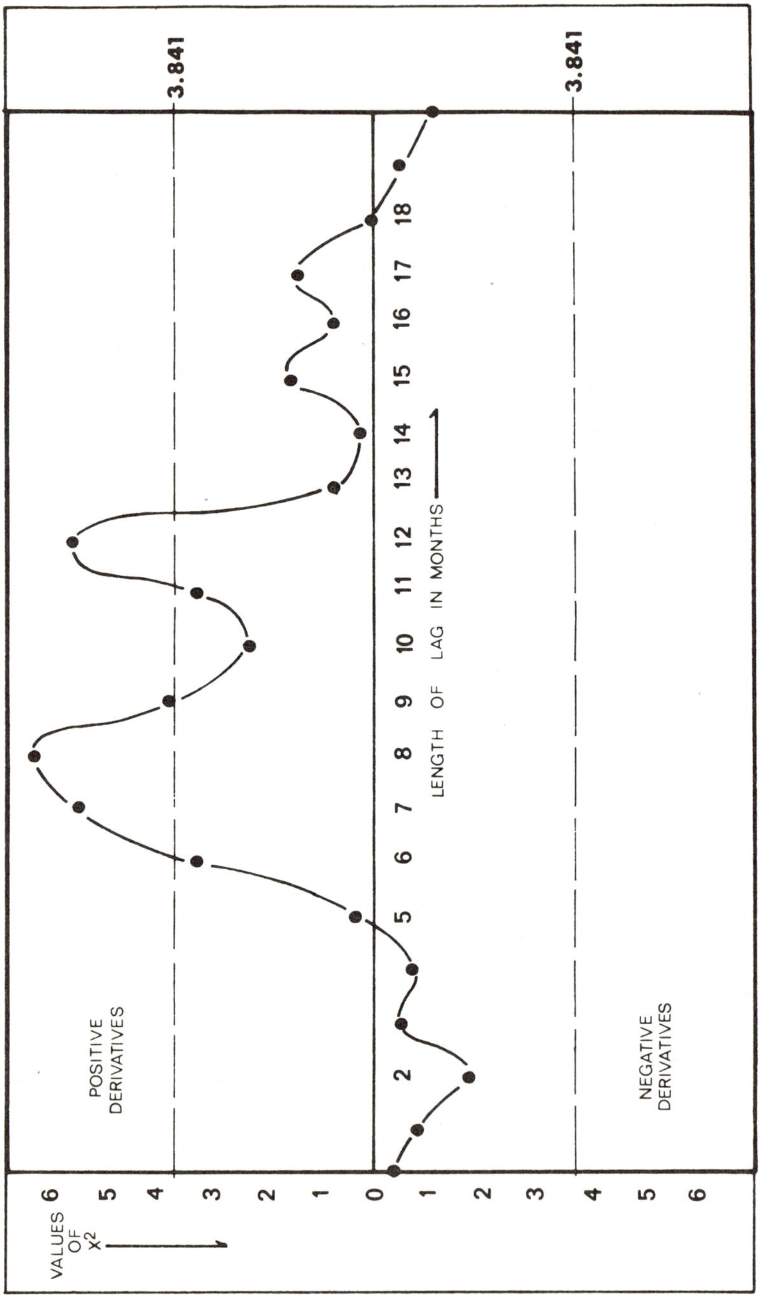

FIG. 6-6. Composite series–monetary restraint.

phenomenon is, as was observed in connection with the production lag analysis, that the policy makers must consider the composite series (or its separate elements) to be an important indicator of the need for stabilization policy action.

As a proxy for income the aggregate economic activity index should move (with a lag) in the same direction as monetary policy, according to the theoretical framework presented. Figures 6-5 and 6-6 confirm this expectation. The number of successes observed for the expansionary series was significant at the 5% alpha level for all lag values from 5 months through 16 months (with the exception of the chi-square value for an 8-month lag which was, however, significant at the 10% level). The chi-square values for the thirteenth and fourteenth lag periods were highest, indicating, probably, a persisting reinforcing effect from the earlier months of strong expansionary policy. Because the composite aggregate index includes four series in addition to industrial production, the occurrence of higher success frequencies later in the period over which the policy effects were distributed may indicate that the added variables have longer average lags than the industrial production series.

For monetary restraint the period over which the lag in effect of monetary policy was distributed appears to have been much shorter (as was the case with the industrial production series). The first chi-square value which was significant at the 5% alpha level appeared in the seventh month after the policy decision. Significant success frequencies appeared in the seventh, eighth, ninth, and twelfth months. Chi-square statistics for the sixth and eleventh months were significant at the 10% alpha level with the value in the tenth month falling slightly below the 10% level. It seems reasonable to conclude that monetary restraint began to be reflected in the composite series in the sixth or seventh month after the policy decision and continued to exert its influence through the twelfth month. For the expansionary series the distributed lag began in the fifth month and extended through the sixteenth month (for the period studied).

The data analysis for the three target variables selected as indicators of the fluctuations in income suggests that real income during the 12-year period between December 1951, and January 1964, was responsive both to expansionary and contractile monetary policy. In the limited framework of the theory presented in Chap. 5 this conclusion would imply that during the period in question the elasticity of nominal wages with respect to the monetary variable was less than unity. Moreover, according to the model, if the elasticity of wages with respect to monetary policy decisions were less than unity, then the elasticity of prices with respect to money must have been so also. And furthermore, a money elasticity of wages of less than unity would imply that the elasticity of interest rates with respect to the monetary variable would be negative. The proxies for wages, prices, and interest rates were introduced into the analysis in an attempt to evaluate these conclusions.

The Lag in Effect on Nominal Wages and Prices

First, the series chosen to represent increases and decreases in the nominal wage was the average hourly earnings of production workers in manufacturing industries as reported in the *Federal Reserve Bulletin.* As a proxy for prices the wholesale commodity price index (also from the *Federal Reserve Bulletin)* was chosen. In each series the first difference from month to month was entered in the position of the later month to form the target vectors. The degree of correspondence of like signs between the monetary policy vector and prices is depicted in Figs. 6-7 and 6-8. The analysis of the effects of monetary policy on nominal wages is described by Figs. 6-9 and 6-10.

The two sequences of 25 consecutive chi-square values below the arbitrarily established significance level as shown by Figs. 6-9 and 6-10 imply that on the basis of the 5% alpha level criterion the null hypotheses cannot be rejected. There is no detectable systematic relationship between the signs of the first differences in the nominal wage and the direction of monetary policy, either expansionary (Fig. 6-9) or contractile (Fig. 6-10).

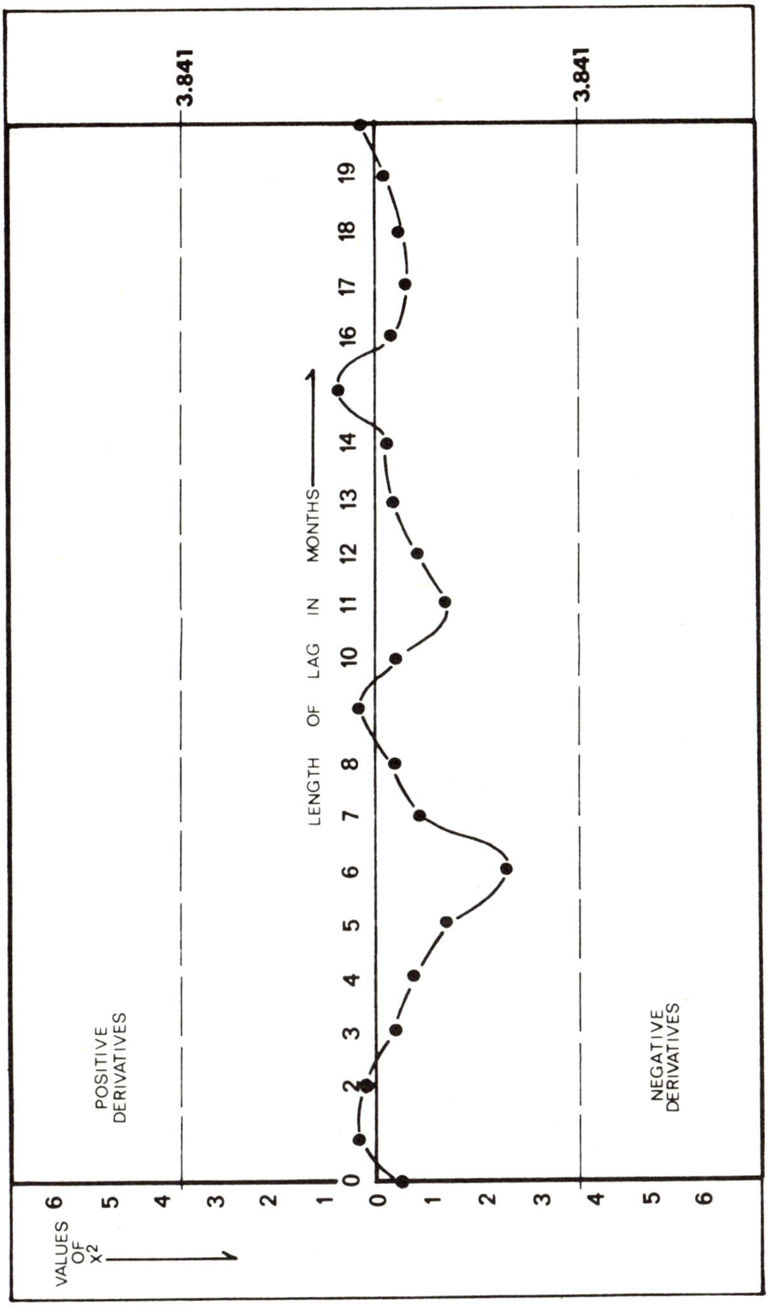

FIG. 6-7. Wholesale prices–monetary expansion.

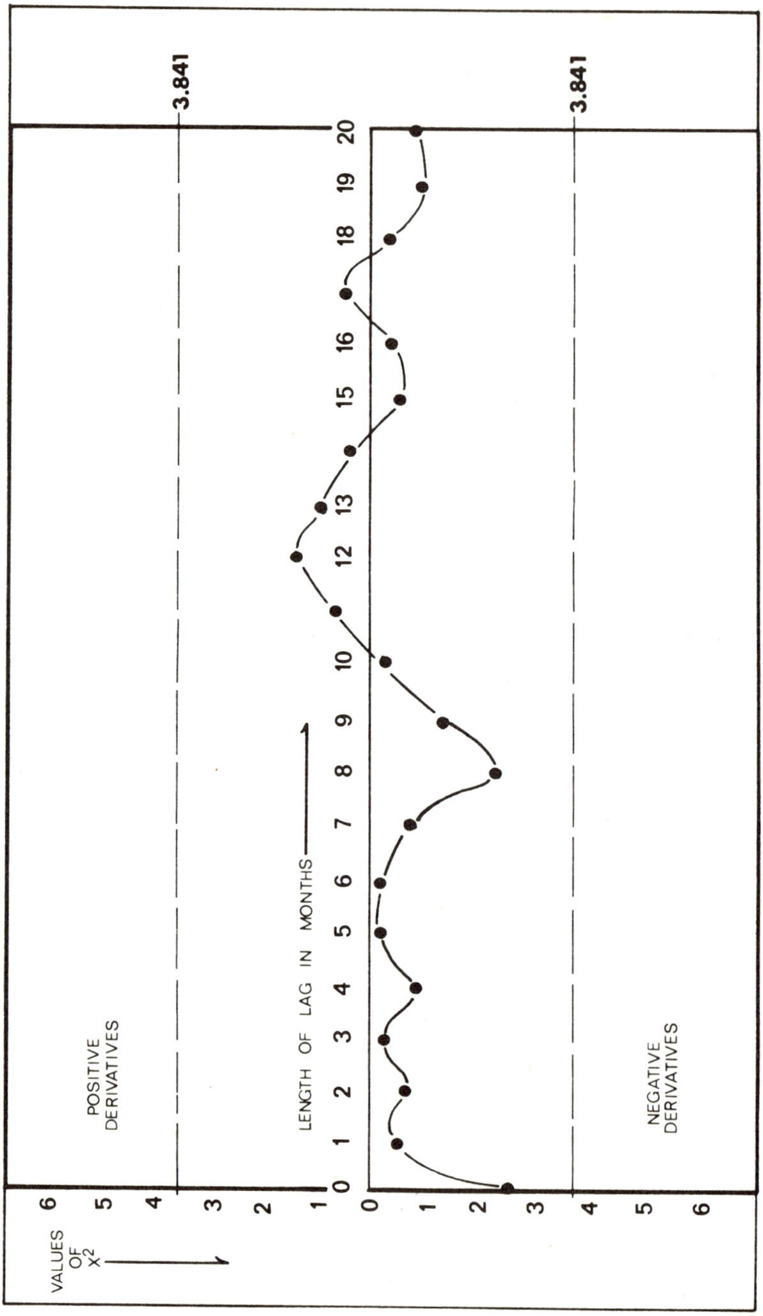

FIG. 6-8. Wholesale prices—monetary restraint.

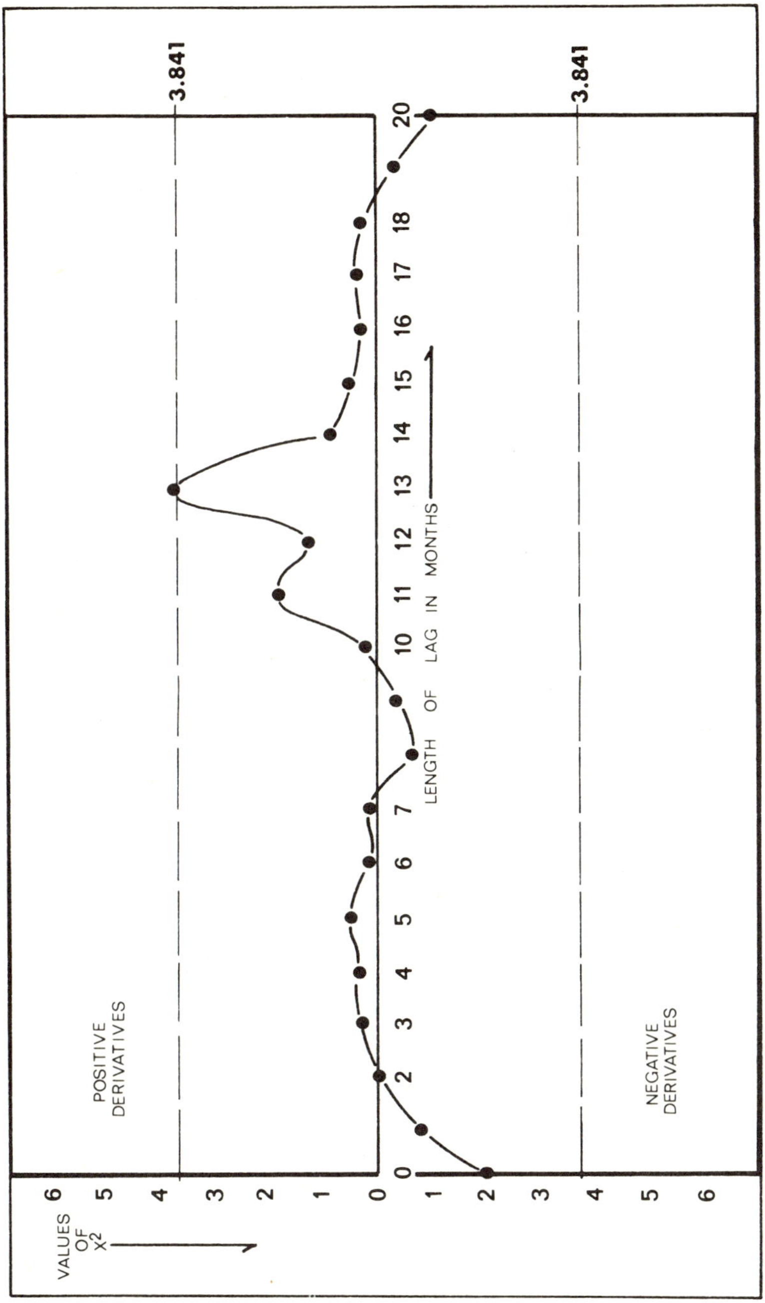

FIG. 6-9. Average hourly wages of production employees–monetary expansion.

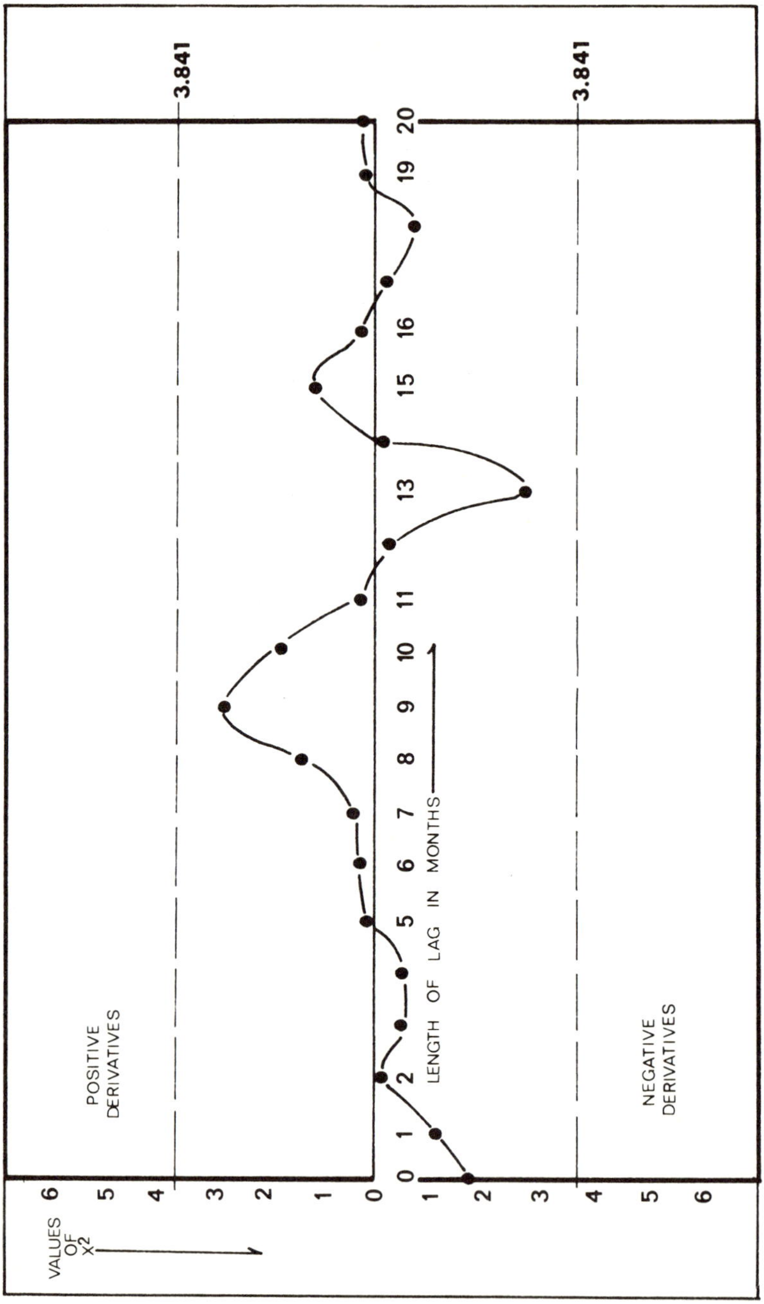

FIG. 6-10. Average hourly wages of production employees–monetary restraint.

The same conclusion holds for the effects of both expansionary monetary policy (Fig. 6-7) and monetary restraint (Fig. 6-8) on the price level.

The fact that there appears to have been a fairly consistent (although not significant for $\alpha = 0.05$) pattern of falling prices in the sixth month after an expansionary policy directive could be rationalized as corresponding (with a short lag) to the falling wages associated with the initiation of expansionary policy and, therefore, as consistent with the theory. Similarly, the observed tendency of wages to rise after a long lag (11 to 13 months according to Fig. 6-9) is not inconsistent with the theory because real output may have risen over the same period at a greater than proportionate rate.

From the standpoint of monetary restraint a similar (and theoretically consistent) pattern can be observed. Rising prices and wages may have been regarded by the monetary authorities as indicators of the need for a retarding monetary policy, hence the higher pattern of "failure" observations at the time of the policy decision. The persistence of rising prices reflected in the peak in the pattern of chi-square values in the eighth month (Fig. 6-8) may reflect the lagged relationship of prices to wages suggested above. In fact, the most significant success frequency in the wage variable (indicating falling wages following a period of monetary restraint) occurred in the ninth month, and the same reaction in the price proxy followed just 3 months later in the twelfth month after monetary restraint. If the small fluctuations in the values of chi square are important indicators, then they seem to confirm the theory. If, on the other hand, all values of chi square which fall below 3.841 are ignored, then both wages and prices may be assumed to have been unresponsive to monetary policy in the period in question and for the proxy variables used.

Neither conclusion is inconsistent with the finding of highly significant responses of real income to monetary policy. The writer chooses to regard wages and prices during the 12-year period covered by the study as relatively unresponsive to the monetary policy decisions made during the period. This position is not only consistent with the statistical criterion established but also with the observation that prices were stable or rising slowly during that interval and wages were rising just about in step with productivity.

Within the theoretical framework presented the sign of the elasticity of interest rates with respect to the money stock was shown to depend on the magnitude of the elasticity of wages minus the elasticity of the marginal productivity of labor both with respect to the money stock so that

$$[e_{WM} - e_{f'(N)M}] \begin{cases} < 1, & \text{then } e_{rM} < 0 \\ = 1, & \text{then } e_{rM} = 0 \\ > 1, & \text{then } e_{rM} > 0 \end{cases}$$

From the preceding analysis it has been concluded that the elasticity of wages with respect to the money stock was less than unity during the period treated in this study; therefore if the interest rate was responsive to monetary policy, the derivative (sign of the first difference) should have been negative according to the theory.

The Lag in Effect on Interest Rates

To test the theory and establish appropriate lag estimates three series were chosen as indicators of the movement of interest rates and credit availability. All three series are reported monthly in the *Federal Reserve Bulletin.* The first interest rate proxy chosen was yields on long term government securities (Figs. 6-11 and 6-12). It was hoped that this series would reflect the variations in government bond prices which occurred due to open market purchases and sales. Free reserves (Figs. 6-13 and 6-14) were selected as an indicator of the relative tightness of credit. The third interest rate-credit availability indicator used was the monthly series of new housing starts (Figs. 6-15 and 6-16).

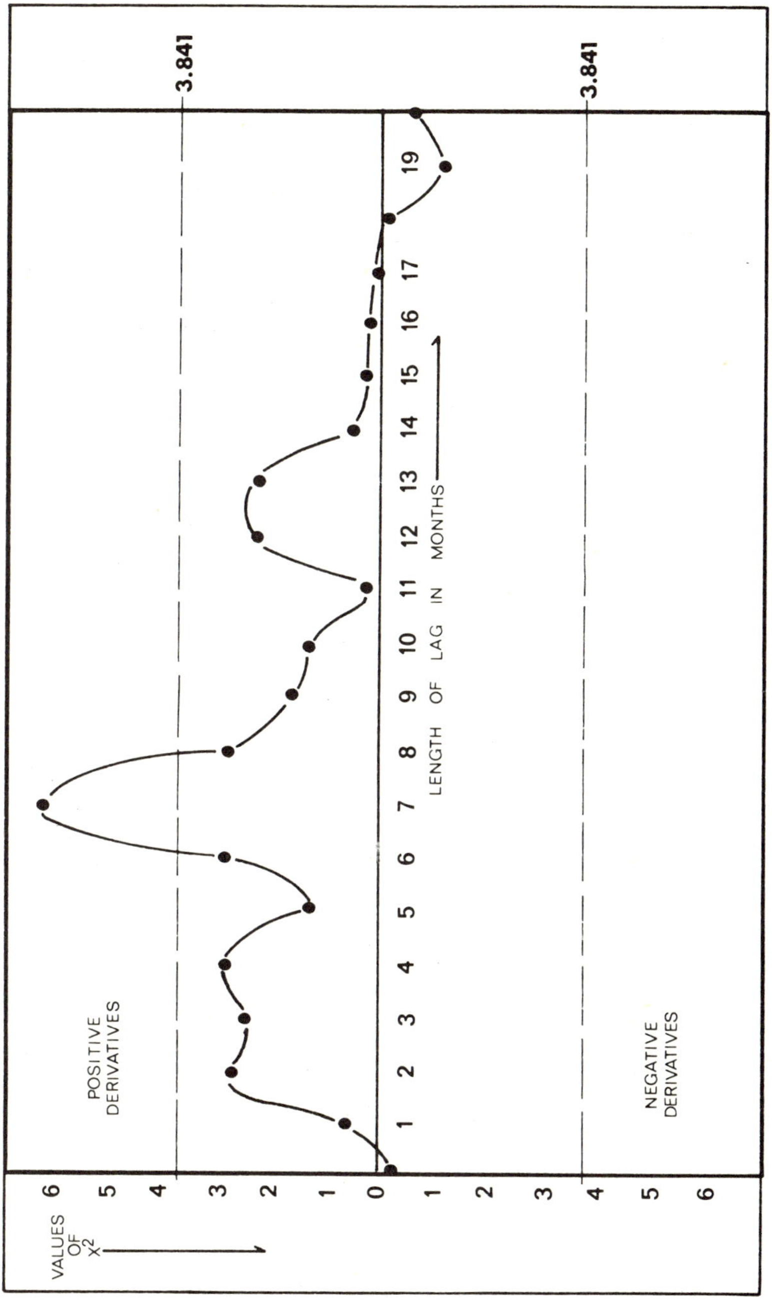

FIG. 6-11. Yields on long-term government bonds–monetary expansion.

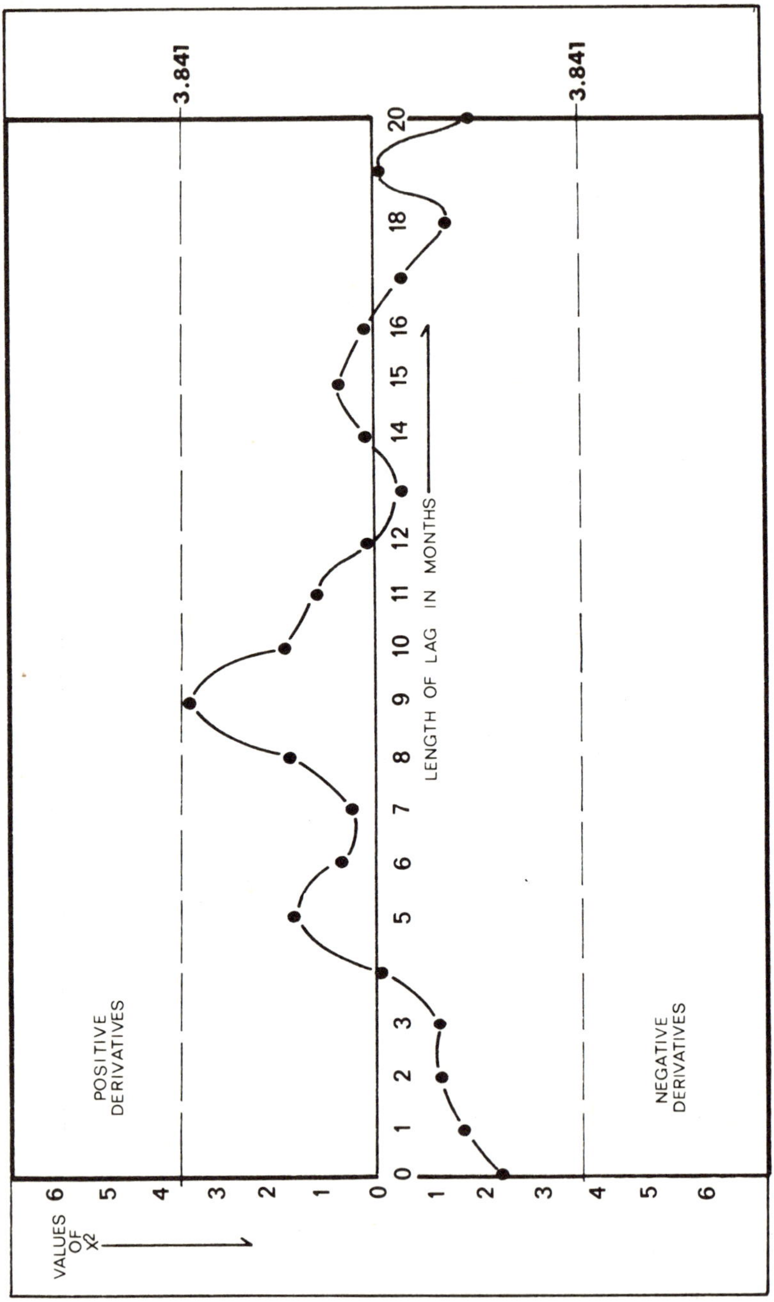

FIG. 6-12. Yields on long-term government bonds–monetary restraint.

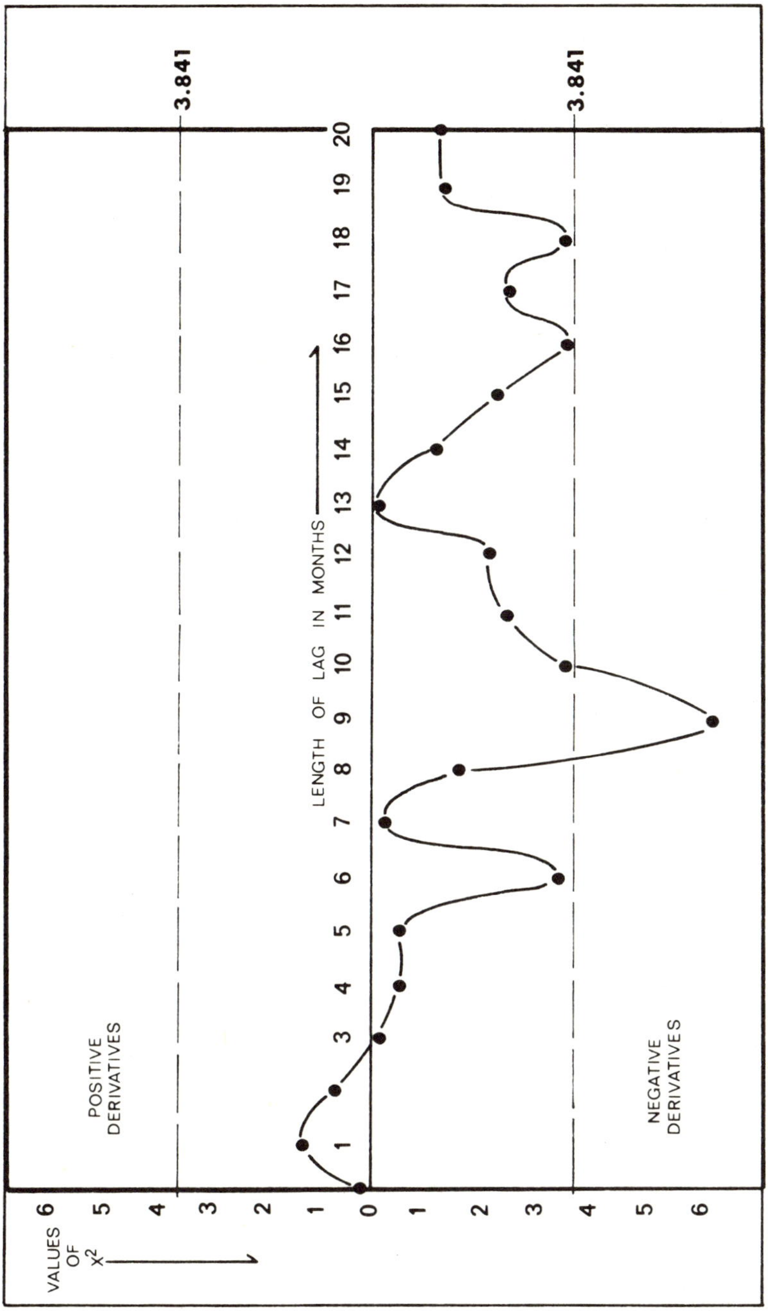

FIG. 6-13. Free reserves–monetary expansion.

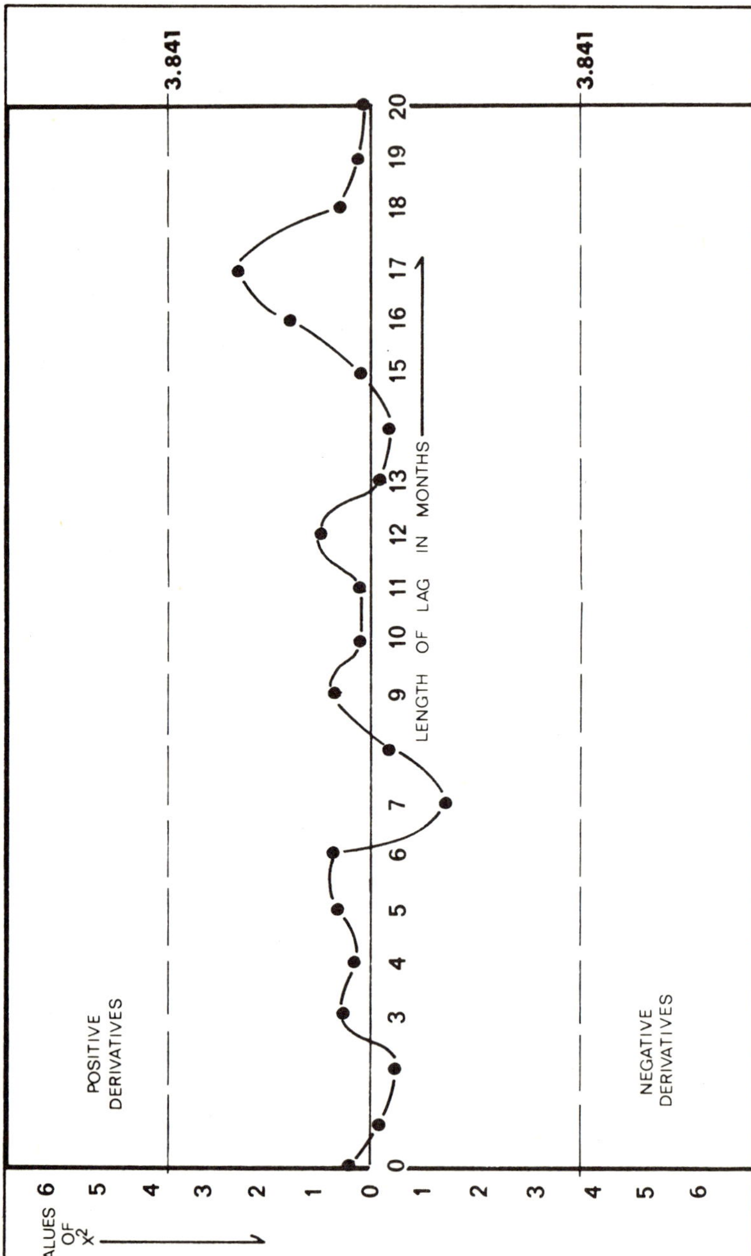

FIG. 6-14. Free reserves–monetary restraint.

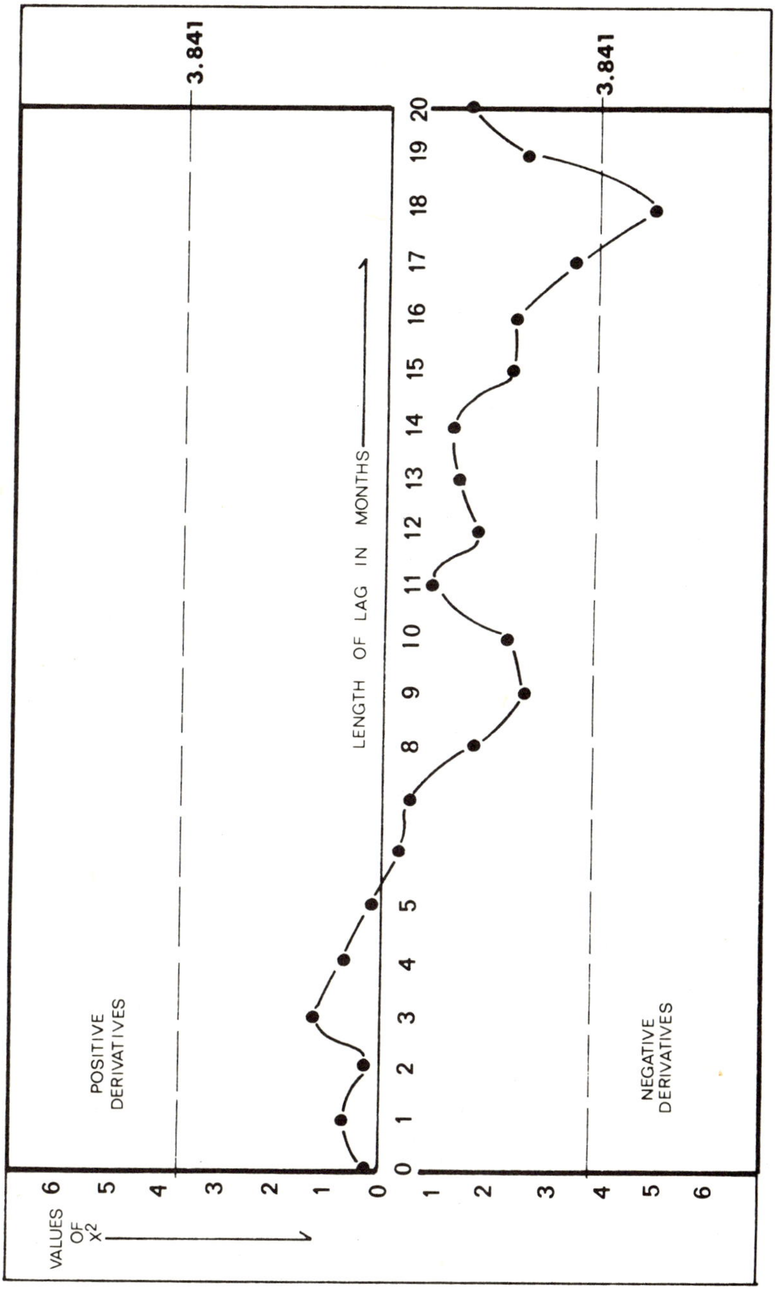

FIG. 6-15. New housing starts–monetary expansion.

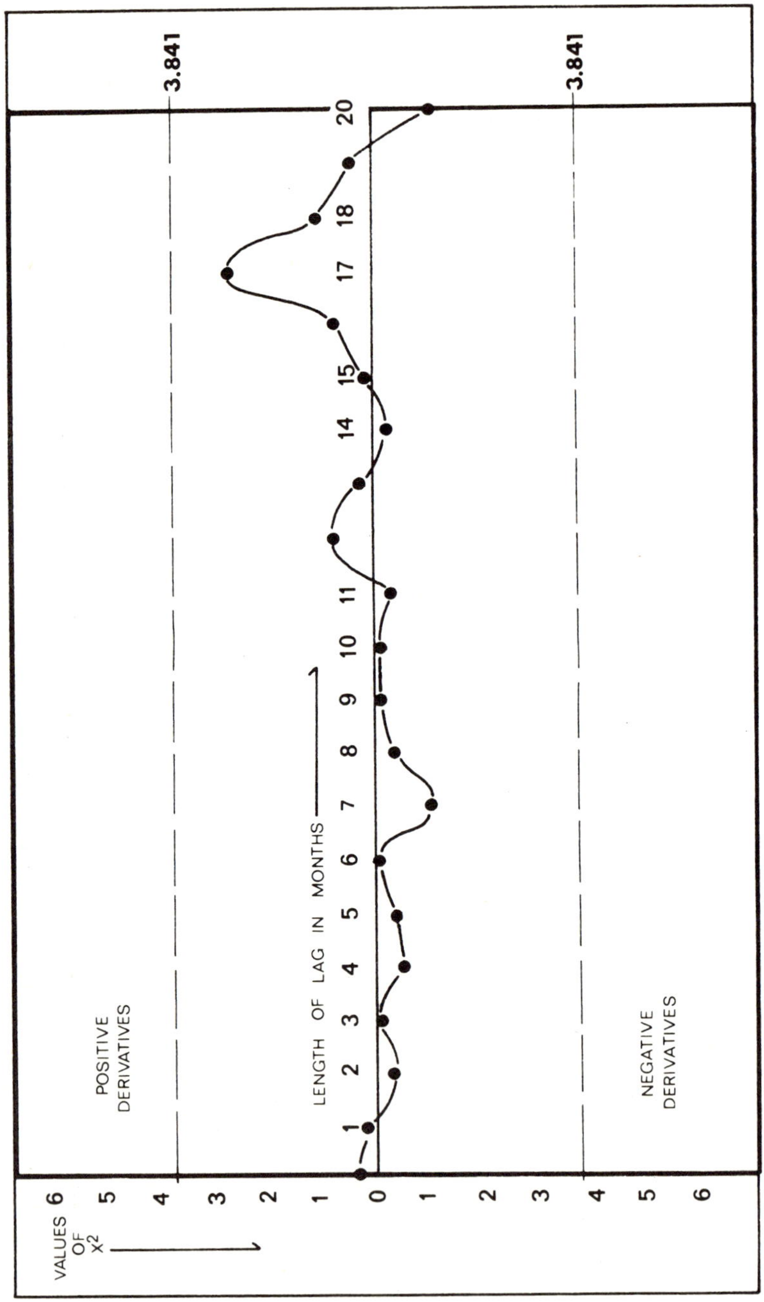

FIG. 6-16. New housing starts—monetary restraint.

If the interest rate variable were responsive to monetary policy decisions, the theory would predict that the bond yields series would move counter to the policy variable. Furthermore, it would be expected that the lag in effect would be relatively short. Figures 6-11 and 6-12 depict the movement of bond yields relative to expansionary and contractile monetary policy decisions, respectively. The immediate and very short-run responses of bond yields to expansionary policy (Fig. 6-11) were not significant. In fact, the only significant success frequency occurred after a lag of 7 months and that in the wrong direction! On the basis of the data relevant to expansionary policy it appears that the expansionary directives not only did not consistently and significantly reduce the bond yields as reported monthly but apparently had the opposite effect after a 7-month lag. The monetary restraint series produced no significant chi-square values for any lag value. With the single exception of the significant "success" frequency in the seventh month of the expansionary series, it would be concluded that yields on long-term government bonds were simply not responsive to monetary policy decisions in the period under consideration. But one highly significant chi-square value did occur (significant at the 1% level) and it should not be neglected. The importance of the observation is reinforced by the fact that the significance levels for the lag periods preceding and following the seventh month are higher than the average of the series. The frequencies for both the sixth and eighth month produced chi-square values which are significant at the 10% probability level.

The distinct pattern of chi-square values in the monetary restraint series (although not significant for $a = 0.05$) provides a hint of a possible explanation of the paradox. Simultaneous with monetary restraint (i.e., lag values 0 through 3 months) interest rates rose with sufficient reliability to produce chi-square values which were significant in the 70-90% probability range. For lag values from the fifth through the twelfth months after monetary restraint the movement in bond yields was downward. The highest chi-square value appeared in the ninth-month lag (significant at $a = 0.10$) with the pattern of chi-square values preceding and following suggesting a systematically increasing then declining influence between the seventh and eleventh months.

If these patterns of success-failure frequencies are important, then the general equilibrium theory of Chap. 5 would appear to be inadequate for the purpose of interpreting the results. The negative first differences observed in the coincident and first 3 months following a decision for monetary restraint indicate rising interest rates, hence are entirely consistent with the theory. But the period of falling interest rates after a 7- to 11-month lag cannot be explained within the assumptions of the model. Similarly, the lack of an immediate significant interest rate decline following an expansionary directive plus the generally rising rates with the peak in success frequencies occurring after a 7-month lag requires explanation from outside the constructs of the model. For the explanation it seems appropriate to incorporate into the model some consideration of expectations.

The theory presented in Chap. 5 was based on an implicit assumption of zero elasticity of expectations with respect to the variables, i.e., when prices or interest rates rise or fall it is not generally taken as an indicator of future fluctuations. The assumption of a positive elasticity of expectations with respect to price rises, for example, would imply that the "representative" decision maker would regard a rise in prices as an indicator that prices will rise in the future. Negative elasticity would mean the opposite: rising prices would be viewed as presaging price declines.

If the elasticity of expectations with respect to the variables of the system is not zero, then the policymakers must consider the possibility that their decisions may have not only the expected direct effects but also some secondary effects reflecting the public's reaction to the induced changes. In the case of expansionary monetary policy, for example, open market purchases of government bonds would be expected to drive bond prices up, bond yields and interest rates down. Bank reserves should rise and credit becomes more readily available. Businessmen would be expected to invest more and consumers presumably would increase installment purchases. But if the freer credit and rising demand should create such an atmosphere of optimism that holders of government securities and other interest-bearing assets became anxious to dispose of their liquid assets in order to make what would appear to be more profitable investments, then securities prices may actually fall. As prices of securities fall and their yields rise, interest rates in general rise as a result of arbitrage; and the effect of expansionary monetary policy on interest rates would seem to have been perverse. Within the framework of the model the preceding discussion implies that the marginal efficiency of capital rose due to expansionary monetary policy and a positive elasticity of expectations with respect to prices and interest rates. A similar argument can be made for the case of monetary restraint.

Judging from the nonsignificant chi-square values for all except one lag period, it does not appear that the expectations effects described were highly consistent during the period from 1952 through 1964. This lack of consistency may reflect a low interest elasticity of the demand for money relative to the interest elasticity of the investment demand function for the period.

The first differences of free reserves followed an interesting pattern relative to the strong monetary stabilization policy intervals identified. (Only one significant chi-square value for $\alpha = 0.05$ appeared; the lag value was 9 months after an expansionary policy decision.) In the expansionary sequence all except the first three lag values reflected preponderately negative first differences (see Figs. 6-13 and 6-14). Within 3 months after a strong expansionary directive free reserves were declining more than half the time. By the sixth month the pattern of falling free reserves was consistent enough to produce a chi-square value which was significant at the 90% probability level. The value in the ninth month was significant at an alpha level of 0.02.

During a period of strong expansionary monetary policy, presumably reserves are growing and, everything else equal, free reserves should be growing also. This was in fact the case in more than half of the observations for each of the lag values, 0 through 2 months. Then the percentage of declining values began the ascent to the significant peak in the ninth month after the policy decision. It appears that the demand for bank loans of acceptable quality was sufficient to induce commercial bankers to continue to lend a substantial part of any increment to excess reserves. This observation is, of course, quite consistent with the earlier discussion of the rising interest rates associated with the expectations effect.

Monetary restraint produced no significant levels of "successes" or "failures" over the entire range of lags from 0 through 24 months. Tight money policy would be expected to reduce total reserves and, temporarily at least, to reduce free reserves also; the data do not reflect any such significant trend. Apparently restrictive monetary policy as identified in this study did not cause banks in the aggregate to adjust the level of free reserves in a manner detectable in the first differences of the monthly data.

The inclusion of new housing starts as an interest rate-credit indicator was an attempt to capture the effects of strong stabilization policies on the important home building sector. With a single exception neither the expansionary nor the contractile series reflected any significant relationship (by the established criterion) between policy decisions and housing starts (see Figs. 6-15 and 6-16). The single exception appeared in the eighteenth month after expansionary policy decisions and indicated a substantial decline in housing starts. (The chi-square value was significant at an alpha level of 0.05.) The housing starts series following expansionary policy may be one case in which the sequence of chi-square values falling below the arbitrarily established criterion should not be disregarded; the pattern of "successes" and "failures" is distinct enough at least to stimulate curiosity.

For the first 5 months after the decision there appear to have been somewhat more frequent increases in housing starts than the trend would have predicted. Then, beginning with the sixth month and continuing through the entire range of lag periods, the frequency of decreases in housing starts was consistently lower than that predicted by the trend. In fact, for $\alpha = 0.10$, both the seventeenth and eighteenth months' chi-square values are significant. If the alpha level were 0.20, then significant values would appear in the eighth-, ninth-, tenth-, and fifteenth- through nineteenth-month lags. In other words the probability is at least 80% in each of the nine instances that the frequency of reductions in housing starts would not have occurred on a purely chance basis.

Although the chi-square values in the earliest lag periods were quite low, the expansion in housing starts on balance is consistent with the theory. Financial organizations whose primary investments are home mortgages would sell some government securities as securities prices rise and increase the proportion of home mortgages in their portfolios. But under certain circumstances this trend could be only temporary. If, as the bond yields and free reserves series indicated, the initial reduction in interest rates reverses after a short period (say 7 months) and optimistic expectations reinforce the demand for bank credit then such institutions as mutual savings banks and savings and loan associations may begin to experience relatively slower growth. In a period of rising interest rates such as that described above, commercial banks can raise the rates charged to their customers much more rapidly than savings and loan associations can raise dividends because of the shorter turnover rate of bank assets. Savings and loan associations are locked into long-term mortgages. Therefore, given the assumed expectations effects and the fact of rising interest rates, the rate of housing starts would be expected to decline.

The periods of monetary restraint during the decade treated in this analysis do not appear to have produced any clearcut trends in the number of housing starts. Perhaps this is due to the relatively short intervals of restraint followed closely by expansionary policy. The effects of expansionary policy appear to have accrued after a long lag following lengthy periods of strong policy directives.

Testing the Lag Estimates on Subsequent Data

The period since 1961 (or, for the target variables, since 1963) has been excluded from this analysis for two reasons. First, and most important, complete minutes of the meetings of the Federal Open Market Committee are not available for the years following 1961; hence the interpretation of recent policy directives is much less reliable. Second, the writer's best evaluation of the Committee's directives since January 1962, indicate only 23 months of strong monetary restraint and 3 months of strong expansionary policy. Eight months of the policy restraint were in the calendar year,

1966, and are clearly associated with the "credit crunch" of 1966-1967. Fourteen months of continuous restraint (as identified by reading the "Record of Policy Actions of the Federal Open Market Committee" section of the *Federal Reserve Bulletin*) began in December 1968, and extended through January 1970. This is by far the longest sustained period of monetary restraint (identified by this writer) since the Treasury-Federal Reserve Accord in 1951. The retarding effects continued at least until late 1970—perhaps even into the spring of 1971, depending upon the choice of indicators. It is too early to make a final assessment of the period. Some observations about the 1960s can, however, be made.

The most dramatic effects of monetary policy identified by this study were in the three series which were chosen as surrogates for real income (output). The results from the wages and prices series were less dramatic but quite consistent with the theory. The three proxies for interest rates (and credit availability) were the most difficult to interpret but suggested certain interesting hypotheses concerning expectations effects. Assuming that the economic system in the period since 1961 is essentially unchanged from that of the previous decade with respect to structural parameters, are the lag estimates from the earlier period consistent with the lags which have occurred since then? For the estimates to be useful for forecasting purposes, separate intervals of strong policy decisions must lead changes in the target variable by approximately the length of the lag established by the analysis described.

Consider the period of monetary restraint which began in February 1966, and lasted through September 1966. The index of industrial production rose in February and in each succeeding month until September when the index fell absolutely (precisely 7 months after the initiation of monetary restraint). The period of restraint lasted for 8 consecutive months; the industrial production series declined in 7 of the 9 months from September 1966, through May 1967. The composite series of aggregate economic activity continued to rise in each successive month after the initiation of monetary restraint until the twelfth month. After a 12-month lag the composite series fell in 5 of the following 9 months. This was the period which has come to be known as the mini-recession of 1967.

Wholesale prices appear to have responded to the monetary restraint of 1966 with a 7-month lag. The 8-month period of restraint began in February and the wholesale price index declined absolutely in September. For the 8-month period from September 1966, through April 1967, the wholesale price index declined each month excepting December and January. During the same period the average hourly wage of production employees appears to have risen and fallen from month to month approximately an equal number of times. Unemployment did not respond with any significant number of increases or decreases, and interest rates continued on the generally upward trend. The number of housing starts had been declining for several consecutive months; this decline continued with the exception of 3 months until February 1967. From the foregoing it appears that the policy restraint of 1966 exerted significant influence on the level of economic activity (as reflected in the industrial production and composite series) with approximately the expected lag, but that the timing of the effects on specific indicators such as wages, interest rates, free reserves, unemployment, and so forth may depend to a large extent on expectations.

To check further the reliability of the forecast of the lag in effect of contractile monetary policy on the economy, consider the period of monetary restraint which began in December 1968, and continued through January 1970. Eight months after the strong policy decision of December 1968, industrial production declined in August 1969, absolutely. It continued to decline in each consecutive month until February 1970. The months of February and March showed net increases and then the index fell again in April. The composite series, reflecting the fluctuations of five "coinciding" indicators, after 22 months of consecutive increases, declined in September 1969. This first reduction in the index in almost 2 years occurred 9 months after the initiation of the policy of strong restraint. Over the next 9 months the series declined five times and remained static for 1 month. The average lag estimates of 7 months for industrial production and 8 months for the composite series do closely approximate the results observed in connection with the two periods of restraint, 1966 and 1969. The third income indicator, unemployment, was estimated to have lagged behind monetary restraint by 7 months on the basis of the complete analysis. Changes in this series did not appear to be significantly correlated with policy decisions in the 1966-1967 period. For the period of monetary restraint beginning in Decmeber 1968, the failure frequency appears to have increased steadily after the first two or three lag periods and continued to rise through the twelfth month. The preliminary conclusion is that the monetary restraint had a significant effect on unemployment after only a short lag.

Wages and prices have responded (if at all) with very long lags to the 1969 period of monetary restraint. The detailed analysis did not establish any clear lag value, so wages and prices (as defined) must be considered either unresponsive to monetary policy or, an alternative possibility, the lags in effects are so highly variable that no consistent pattern can be identified from the first differences. In either case, efforts to stabilize prices in the short run through countercyclical monetary policy appear futile. This conclusion, of course, does not necessarily imply that monetary policy cannot be used to promote price stability over longer periods. In the following final chapter of this book, the policy implications of these results will be discussed.

Monetary Policy and Economic Stability

The Empirical Results Interpreted in the Theoretical Context of Chapter 5

The nonparametric analysis reported in the preceding chapter disclosed significant effects of strong monetary policy directives on real income accruing after a comparatively short lag. According to the theory developed in Chap. 5, a positive elasticity of real income with respect to the money stock would be associated with money supply elasticities of nominal wages and prices ranging downward from unity. The empirical analysis of Chap. 6 is completely consistent with the theory in this respect. To be consistent with these findings, the elasticity of interest rates with respect to the monetary variable should be negative. Again, the data confirmed (or failed to disprove) the theory in this respect for very short lag values (less than 3 months). After a short period the derivatives of the rate of interest with respect to earlier monetary policy decisions became positive, a development most easily explained by the assumption that the elasticity of expectations with respect to prices and interest rates was greater than zero. Assuming that the theoretical constructs of Chap. 5 are consonant with the workings of the economic system, the conclusions of this analysis have certain policy implications.

Discretionary Monetary Policy and the Price Level

The relatively low significance levels which were generated for all lag values when testing for the effects of discretionary stabilization policy decisions of the monetary authorities on nominal wages and prices can be explained in a number of ways. An obvious interpretation is the theoretical one cited in the first paragraph of this chapter. It could be argued, alternatively, that institutional rigidities in wage and price structures may preclude the identification of any regularity in response to monetary policy decisions. Wages, for example, are in many cases established by contract for long periods in advance so that the absence of an immediate response may obscure a quite powerful response to monetary policy. Even those wage changes not predetermined by union contract may be made predominantly on a regular and infrequent basis. Similarly, prices of most products, once established, generally remain static over relatively long periods because of the costs associated with changing posted and published prices. Furthermore, government intervention in the form of subsidies and price supports tends to mitigate the market pressures which would otherwise bring about price adjustments. Still another rationale which fits the empirical findings is the argument of some monetarists: the effects of discretionary stabilization policy decisions of the monetary authorities are very powerful but the lags in effect on prices, for example, are so highly variable that efforts at price stabilization through monetary policy are apt to be ineffective or counterproductive.

The interesting aspect of these arguments is that they all point to the same conclusion: discretionary monetary policy cannot be considered to be a reliable tool for the promotion of price stability in the short run. The results of this study indicate that efforts to halt a given inflationary spiral with strong monetary restraint will inevitably succeed first in reducing income, output, and employment. If monetary restraint were extended over a long period, prices would eventually cease to rise but the levels of unemployment which would accompany the result might prove to be unacceptable. Is promotion of price stability, then, not a proper function of monetary policy? A brief review of the theoretical construct is instructive in this respect.

Prices and output are ultimately determined, according to the general equilibrium model of Chap. 5, by the interaction of aggregate demand and aggregate supply. If, for any reason, there is a shift in aggregate demand such that the quantities demanded at all possible prices are greater after the shift, then both the equilibrium price and quantity should rise. How much each rises is determined by the relative elasticities of demand and supply with respect to price. Under the assumption of diminishing marginal productivity, the price elasticity of supply for a given nominal wage is high for low levels of employment and low for levels of output associated with full employment (or very low levels of unemployment). Accordingly, demand shifts during periods of full employment should produce substantial price effects and negligible effects on output. Shifts in demand which occur when unemployment is high should produce the opposite results.

The elasticity of aggregate demand depends jointly on the elasticity of demand for money balances with respect to interest rates and the interest elasticity of investment (and consumption) demand. Highly interest-elastic investment demand functions are associated with high price elasticities of aggregate demand. Low interest elasticities of demand for money are associated with high price elasticities of aggregate demand. Low interest elasticities of demand for money are associated with high price elasticities of aggregate demand. The model, therefore, would predict higher aggregate demand price elasticities for higher levels of output and the converse. Consequently, a shift in the supply schedule such that the quantities supplied at all possible prices were lower than previously would imply a substantial reduction in output and a negligible increase in prices under conditions approaching full employment, the reverse for periods of high unemployment.

The period covered by this study was one in which unemployment fluctuated perceptibly at low levels to be sure compared with those of severe recessionary intervals but at relatively high levels compared to those of the late 1960s. The effects of strong countercyclical monetary policy decisions on output proved to be significant in terms of the empirical tests described in Chap. 6. Prices, on the other hand, did not appear to respond reliably. This result is, again, consistent with the theory in Chap. 5 if the period in question can be described as predominantly one of underutilization of resources. Expansionary monetary policy, then, may be effective as a stimulus to demand and, hence, an efficacious weapon against unemployment. Monetary restraint should be an adequate weapon against inflation under conditions of full employment, but for a variety of reasons the response of prices to falling aggregate demand may lag behind that of output so that high levels of unemployment may precede price declines.

Policy Recommendations

The empirical results reported in Chap. 6 imply that the effects of strong countercyclical monetary policy decisions on real output and on business conditions generally begin to accrue after a short lag (perhaps 6 to 8 months or less). The tests showed that the effects were distributed over several months (perhaps 6 to 10 months) and that the length of the lag from decision to effect on output was reasonably consistent. Wages and prices did not respond significantly according to the stringent test criteria established. Apparently discretionary monetary policy has asymmetric effects.

Monetary restraint increases unemployment in the short run; expansionary monetary actions cause (or permit) inflation in a long-run context.

Some economists have advocated the government's pursuing an "incomes policy" so that inflation might be restrained and unemployment minimized simultaneously. Such policy recommendations encompass possibilities ranging from the Kennedy Administration's wage and price guidelines to the Nixon Administration's wage and price freeze. Policies of the kind in question have been more or less effective in the short run—consistently unenforceable and ineffective in the long run[1]. Furthermore, the stresses which are built into an economy so controlled almost certainly complicate the adjustment processes involved in any movement toward stability. Incomes policies are generally viewed as instruments of last resort, their implementation implying not only that economic conditions are unacceptable but that the efforts of the policy makers to "fine tune" the economy have failed. Eschewing, therefore, such drastic prescriptions, can economists recommend a workable program for economic stability? Professor Friedman has suggested a system of rules by which the monetary authorities would be charged with the responsibility for engineering a predetermined growth rate in the money stock (however defined) approximately equal to the long-term growth rate of the level of real output. The reasoning behind this proposal is that the effect would be not only to promote price stability in the long run but also an atmosphere of confidence among businessmen concerning the availability of credit. In view of the results of this analysis, Friedman's proposal is most attractive. If discretionary monetary policy is destined to produce inflation or unemployment (or both) then perhaps an inflexible rule would reduce economic instability. Certainly if all cyclical fluctuations in the level of economic activity could be attributed to the perversities of discretionary monetary policy, then the argument for rules would be compelling.

However, it has been argued in this book that the Federal Reserve has engaged in strong anticyclical activities only occasionally and that much of the cyclic behavior of the money stock has been unrelated to open market purchases and sales of government securities. There are many actions which commercial bankers can take to cause the level of reserves and credit to rise or fall in the absence of offsetting actions by the Federal Reserve. Similarly, a variety of actions initiated solely by the public (households and businesses) can cause the level of credit to change. Not only is it misleading to use fluctuations in the money stock as an indicator of the timing of countercyclical monetary policy actions, it is incorrect to associate all inflations and recessions with active monetary policy decisions. If the monetary authorities are to be blamed for the peaks and troughs of the business cycle, it must be in many cases precisely because of their failure to act.

The evidence indicates that the Federal Open Market Committee can promote economic stability by utilizing its discretionary powers to counter the effects of the unmanaged determinants of the money stock. The primary objective should be to minimize the deviations of the money stock about some appropriate long-term growth rate. Secondarily, to promote price stability, the growth rate of the money stock should be set equal to the growth rate of real output.

The prescription for a constant growth rate of the money stock running counter to cyclic fluctuations of the economy is not economically irresponsible. At some point the cost of inflation in terms of declining real balances and excessive debt maintenance costs will exceed the total cost of transfer payments to the unemployed. As the public becomes more sophisticated concerning the economics of inflation and less phrenetic in regard to unemployment compensation, the use of a consistent monetary policy rule to stabilize prices may prove to be both effective and politically feasible.

Note

1. Lloyd Ulman and Robert J. Flanagan, *Wage Restraint: A Study of Incomes Policies in Western Europe* (Berkeley: University of California Press, 1971).

Appendix

Summary: Prevailing Policy Actions of the Federal Open Market Committee of the Federal Reserve System—January, 1952 through December, 1969

Year	Jan.	Feb.	Mar.	Apr.	May	June	July	Aug.	Sept.	Oct.	Nov.	Dec.
1952	0	0	0	0	0	0	0	0	0	0	−1	−1
1953	−1	−1	−1	−1	−1	0	0	0	0	+1	+1	+1
1954	+1	+1	+1	+1	+1	+1	+1	+1	+1	+1	+1	+1
1955	0	0	0	0	0	0	0	0	0	0	0	0
1956	0	0	0	−1	−1	0	0	−1	−1	−1	−1	0
1957	0	0	0	−1	−1	−1	−1	−1	0	0	0	+1
1958	+1	+1	+1	+1	+1	+1	+1	+1	+1	+1	+1	+1
1959	0	0	0	0	0	0	0	0	0	0	0	0
1960	0	0	0	0	0	+1	+1	+1	+1	+1	+1	+1
1961	+1	+1	+1	+1	+1	+1	+1	+1	+1	+1	+1	+1
1962	0	0	0	0	0	0	0	0	0	0	0	0
1963	0	0	0	0	0	0	0	0	0	0	0	0
1964	0	0	0	0	0	0	0	0	0	0	0	0
1965	0	0	0	−1	0	0	0	0	0	0	0	0
1966	0	−1	−1	−1	−1	−1	−1	−1	−1	0	0	0
1967	0	+1	+1	+1	0	0	0	0	0	0	0	0
1968	0	0	0	0	0	0	0	0	0	0	0	−1
1969	−1	−1	−1	−1	−1	−1	−1	−1	−1	−1	−1	−1

An Interpretation of the Policy Decisions of the Federal Open Market Committee

Year	Date	Rank	Month	Value
		Primary Period		
			January	0
1952	2-29	+1	February	0
	3-1	−1	March	0
	4-4	−1		
	4-21	−1	April	0
	5-9	−1		
	5-23	−1	May	0
	6-6	−1		
	6-19	−1	June	0
	7-22	−1	July	0
	8-29	−1	August	0
	9-15	−1		
	9-25	−1	September	0
	10-8	−1		
	10-22	−1	October	0
	11-5	−2		
	11-25	−2	November	−1
	12-8	−2		
	12-23	−2	December	−1
1953	1-6	−2		
	1-27	−2	January	−1
	2-10	−2	February	−1
	3-5	−2		
	3-24	−2	March	−1
	4-8	−3		
	4-24	−3	April	−1
	5-6	−3		
	5-13	−2		
	5-26	−2	May	−1
	6-11	−1		
	6-11	−1		
	6-23	+1	June	0

Year	Date	Rank	Month	Value
1953	7-7	+1		
	7-21	+1	July	0
	8-4	+1		
	8-25	+1	August	0
	9-8	+1		
	9-24	+2	September	0
	10-6	+2		
	10-20	+2	October	+1
	11-6	+2		
	11-23	+2	November	+1
	12-15	+3	December	+1
1954	1-5	+3		
	1-19	+3	January	+1
	2-2	+3		
	2-17	+3	February	+1
	3-3	+3		
	3-16	+3		
	3-30	+3	March	+1
	4-13	+3		
	4-27	+3	April	+1
	5-11	+3		
	5-26	+3	May	+1
	6-8	+3		
	6-23	+3	June	+1
	7-7	+3		
	7-20	+4	July	+1
	8-3	+4		
	8-24	+4	August	+1
	9-8	+4		
	9-22	+3	September	+1
	10-5	+3		
	10-20	+3	October	+1
	11-9	+3		
	11-23	+3	November	+1
	12-7	+3		
	12-28	+3	December	+1

Year	Date	Rank	Month	Value
1955	1-11	+1		
	1-25	+1	January	0
	2-8	+1	February	0
	3-2	+1		
	3-29	+1	March	0
	4-12	+1		
	4-26	+1	April	0
	5-10	+1		
	5-24	+1	May	0
	6-6	+1		
	6-22	+1	June	0
	7-12	+1	July	0
	8-2	−1		
	8-23	−1	August	0
	9-14	−1	September	0
	10-4	−1		
	10-25	−1	October	0
	11-16	−1		
	11-30	−1	November	0
	12-8	−1		
	12-13	−1	December	0
1956	1-10	−1		
	1-24	−1	January	0
	2-15	−1	February	0
	3-6	−1		
	3-27	−2	March	0
	4-17	−2	April	−1
	5-9	−2		
	5-23	−1	May	−1
	6-5	−1		
	6-26	−1	June	0
	7-17	−1	July	0
	8-7	−2		
	8-21	−2	August	−1
	9-11	−2		
	9-25	−2	September	−1
	10-16	−2	October	−1

Year	Date	Rank	Month	Value
1956	11-13	−2		
	11-27	−1	November	−1
	12-10	−1	December	0
1957	1-8	−1		
	1-28	−1	January	0
	2-18	−1	February	0
	3-5	−1		
	3-26	−2	March	0
	4-16	−2		
	4-24	−2	April	−1
	5-7	−2		
	5-28	−2	May	−1
	6-18	−2	June	−1
	7-9	−2		
	7-30	−2	July	−1
	8-20	−2	August	−1
	9-10	−1	September	0
	10-1	−1		
	10-22	−1	October	0
	11-12	+1	November	0
	12-3	+2		
	12-17	+3	December	+1
1958	1-7	+3		
	1-28	+3	January	+1
	2-11	+3	February	+1
	3-4	+4		
	3-25	+4	March	+1
	4-15	+4	April	+1
	5-6	+4		
	5-27	+4	May	+1
	6-17	+4	June	+1
	7-8	+4		
	7-15	+4		
	7-18	+5		
	7-21	+5		
	7-22	+4		

Year	Date	Rank	Month	Value
1958	7-23	+4		
	7-23	+4		
	7-25	+4		
	7-29	−1		
	7-31	−1	July	+1
	8-1	−1		
	8-4	−1		
	8-19	+2	August	+1
	9-9	+2		
	9-30	+2	September	+1
	10-21	+2	October	+1
	11-10	+2	November	+1
	12-2	+2		
	12-16	+1	December	+1
1959	1-6	+1		
	1-27	+1	January	0
	2-10	+1	February	0
	3-3	+1		
	3-24	+1	March	0
	4-14	+1	April	0
	5-5	+1		
	5-26	−1	May	0
	6-16	−1	June	0
	7-7	−1		
	7-28	−1	July	0
	8-18	−1	August	0
	9-1	−1		
	9-22	−1	September	0
	10-13	−1	October	0
	11-4	−1		
	11-24	−1	November	0
	12-15	−1	December	0
1960	1-12	+1		
	1-26	+1	January	0
	2-9	+1	February	0
	3-1	+1		

Year	Date	Rank	Month	Value
1960	3-22	+1	March	0
	4-12	+1	April	0
	5-3	+1		
	5-24	+2	May	0
	6-14	+2	June	+1
	7-6	+2		
	7-26	+2	July	+1
	8-16	+2	August	+1
	9-13	+3	September	+1
	10-4	+3		
	10-25	+3	October	+1
	11-22	+3	November	+1
	12-13	+3	December	+1
1961	1-10	+3		
	1-24	+3	January	+1
	2-7	+3	February	+1
	3-7	+3		
	3-28	+3	March	+1
	4-18	+4	April	+1
	5-9	+4	May	+1
	6-6	+4		
	6-20	+4	June	+1
	7-11	+4	July	+1
	8-1	+4		
	8-22	+3	August	+1
	9-12	+3	September	+1
	10-3	+3		
	10-24	+3	October	+1
	11-14	+3	November	+1
	12-5	+3		
	12-19	+3	December	+1
		Secondary Period		
1962	1-9	+1		
	1-23	+1	January	0
	2-13	+1	February	0
	3-6	+1		

Year	Date	Rank	Month	Value
1962	3-27	+1	March	0
	4-17	+1	April	0
	5-8	+1		
	5-29	+1	May	0
	6-19	−1		
	6-21	−1	June	0
	7-10	+1		
	7-31	+1	July	0
	8-21	−1	August	0
	9-11	−1	September	0
	10-2	+1		
	10-23	+1	October	0
	11-13	+1	November	0
	12-4	+1		
	12-18	+1	December	0
1963	1-8	−1		
	1-29	−1	January	0
	2-12	−1	February	0
	3-5	−1		
	3-26	−1	March	0
	4-16	−1	April	0
	5-7	−2*		
	5-28	−1	May	0
	6-18	−1	June	0
	7-9	−1		
	7-30	−2*	July	0
	8-20	−1	August	0
	9-10	−1	September	0
	10-1	−1		
	10-22	−1	October	0
	11-12	−1		
	11-26	−1	November	0
	12-3	−1		
	12-17	+1	December	0

*Isolated strong instructions have been assigned zero values.

Year	Date	Rank	Month	Value
1964	1-7	+1		
	1-28	+1	January	0
	2-11	+1	February	0
	3-3	+1		
	3-24	+1	March	0
	4-14	+1	April	0
	5-5	+1		
	5-26	+1	May	0
	6-17	+1	June	0
	7-7	+1		
	7-28	+1	July	0
	8-18	−1	August	0
	9-8	−1		
	9-29	−1	September	0
	10-20	−1	October	0
	11-10	−1		
	11-24	−1	November	0
	12-1	+1		
	12-15	+1	December	0
1965	1-12	+1	January	0
	2-2	−1	February	0
	3-2	−1		
	3-23	−2	March	0
	4-13	−2	April	−1
	5-11	−1		
	5-25	−1	May	0
	6-15	−1	June	0
	7-13	−1	July	0
	8-10	−1		
	8-31	−1	August	0
	9-8	−1		
	9-28	−1	September	0
	10-12	−1	October	0
	11-2	−1		
	11-23	−1	November	0
	12-14	−1	December	0

Year	Date	Rank	Month	Value
1966	1-11	−1	January	0
	2-8	−2	February	−1
	3-1	−2		
	3-22	−2	March	−1
	4-12	−2	April	−1
	5-10	−2	May	−1
	6-7	−2		
	6-28	−2	June	−1
	7-26	−2	July	−1
	8-23	−2	August	−1
	9-13	−2	September	−1
	10-4	−1	October	0
	11-1	−1		
	11-22	+1	November	0
	12-13	+1	December	0
1967	1-10	+1	January	0
	2-7	+2	February	+1
	3-7	+2	March	+1
	4-4	+2	April	+1
	5-2	+1		
	5-23	+1	May	0
	6-20	+1	June	0
	7-18	+1	July	0
	8-15	+1	August	0
	9-12	+1	September	0
	10-3	+1		
	10-24	+1	October	0
	11-14	+1		
	11-27	+1	November	0
	12-12	−1	December	0
1968	1-9	−1	January	0
	2-6	−1	February	0
	3-5	−1		
	3-14	−1	March	0
	4-2	−1		

Year	Date	Rank	Month	Value
1968	4-19	–1		
	4-30	–1	April	0
	5-28	–1	May	0
	6-18	–1	June	0
	7-16	+1	July	0
	8-13	+1		
	8-19	+1	August	0
	9-10	+1	September	0
	10-8	+1		
	10-24	+1	October	0
	11-26	+1	November	0
	12-17	–3	December	–1
1969	1-14	–2	January	–1
	2-4	–2	February	–1
	3-4	–2	March	–1
	4-1	–1		
	4-29	–2	April	–1
	5-27	–2	May	–1
	6-24	–3	June	–1
	7-15	–4	July	–1
	8-12	–3	August	–1
	9-9	–3	September	–1
	10-7	–2		
	10-28	–3	October	–1
	11-25	–2	November	–1
	12-16	–2	December	–1

Bibliography

Books

Bailey, Martin J. *National Income and the Price Level.* New York: McGraw-Hill, 1962.

Bradley, James V. *Distribution-Free Statistical Tests.* Englewood Cliffs, N.J.: Prentice-Hall, Inc., 1968.

Christ, Carl F. *Econometric Models and Methods.* New York: John Wiley and Sons, Inc., 1966.

Commission on Money and Credit. *Stabilization Policies.* Englewood Cliffs, N.J.: Prentice-Hall, Inc., 1963.

Draper, N.R., and H. Smith. *Applied Regression Analysis.* New York: John Wiley & Sons, Inc., 1966.

Duncan, Acheson J. *Quality Control and Industrial Statistics.* Homewood, Ill.: Richard D. Irwin, Inc., 1965.

Evans, Michael, and Lawrence Klein. *The Wharton Econometric Forecasting Model.* Philadelphia: Wharton School of Finance and Commerce, University of Pennsylvania, 1967.

Friedman, Milton. *Essays in Positive Economics.* Chicago: University of Chicago Press, 1953.

_________ "A Monetary and Fiscal Framework for Economic Stability." In Fredrich A. Lutz and Lloyd W. Mints, eds., *Readings in Monetary Theory.* Homewood, Ill.: Richard D. Irwin, Inc., 1951.

_________ *The Optimum Quantity of Money and Other Essays.* Chicago: Aldine Publishing Co., 1969.

_________ *A Program for Monetary Stability.* New York: Fordham University Press, 1959.

_________ and David Meiselman. "The Relative Stability of Monetary Velocity and the Investment Multiplier in the United States, 1897-1958." In Commission on Money and Credit, *Stabilization Policies.* Englewood Cliffs, N.J.: Prentice-Hall, Inc., 1963.

_________ and Anna J. Schwartz. *A Monetary History of the United States, 1867-1960.* Princeton: Princeton University Press, 1963.

Green, H.A. John. *Aggregation in Economic Analysis.* Princeton, N.J.: Princeton University Press, 1964.

Harberger, Arnold C. "The Dynamics of Inflation in Chile." In Carl Christ, *et. al.*, eds., *Measurement in Economics.* Stanford, Calif.: Stanford University Press, 1963.

Hendershott, Patric H. *The Neutralized Money Stock.* Homewood, Ill.: Richard D. Irwin, Inc., 1968.

Horvitz, Paul M. *Monetary Policy and the Financial System.* 2nd ed. rev. Englewood Cliffs, N.J.: Prentice-Hall, Inc., 1969.

Johnston, J. *Econometric Methods.* New York: McGraw-Hill, 1963.

Kane, Edward J. *Economic Statistics and Econometrics.* New York: Harper and Row, 1968.

Kareken, John, and Robert M. Solow. "Lags in Monetary Policy." In Commission on Money and Credit, ed., *Stabilization Policies.* Englewood Cliffs, N.J.: Prentice-Hall, Inc., 1963.

Kendall, Maurice G., and Alan Stuart. *The Advanced Theory of Statistics.* Vol. 3. New York: Hafner Publishing Company, 1966.

Landes, David S. *The Unbound Prometheus.* Cambridge: Cambridge University Press, 1969.

Lutz, Fredrich A., and Lloyd W. Mints, eds., *Readings in Monetary Theory.* Homewood, Ill.: Richard D. Irwin, Inc., 1951.

Mayer, Thomas. "The Inflexibility of Monetary Policy." In Richard S. Thorn, ed., *Monetary Theory and Policy.* New York: Random House, 1966.

_________ *Monetary Policy in the United States.* New York: Random House, 1968.

Siegel, Sidney. *Nonparametric Statistics for the Behavioral Sciences.* New York: McGraw-Hill, 1956.

Simons, Henry C. "Rule Versus Authority in Monetary Policy." In Fredrich A. Lutz and Lloyd W. Mints, eds., *Readings in Monetary Theory.* Homewood, Ill.: Richard D. Irwin, Inc., 1951.

Slutsky, Eugen E. "On the Theory of the Budget of the Consumer." In George J. Stigler and Kenneth E. Boulding, eds., *Readings in Price Theory.* Homewood, Ill.: Richard D. Irwin, Inc., 1952.

Thorn, Richard S., ed. *Monetary Theory and Policy.* New York: Random House, 1966.

Ulman, Lloyd, and Robert J. Flanagan. *Wage Restraint: A Study of Incomes Policies in Western Europe.* Berkeley: University of California Press, 1971.

Walsh, John E. *Handbook of Nonparametric Statistics.* Vol. 1. New York: D. Van Nostrand Company, Inc., 1962.

Wicker, Elmus R. *Federal Reserve Monetary Policy 1917-1933.* New York: Random House, 1966.

Wonnacott, Ronald J., and Thomas H. Wonnacott. *Econometrics.* New York: John Wiley & Sons, Inc., 1970.

Articles and Periodicals

Anderson, Leonall C., and Jerry L. Jordan. "Monetary and Fiscal Actions: A Test of Their Relative Importance in Economic Stabilization." Reprint from *Review,* Federal Reserve Bank of St. Louis, 34 (November 1968).

Bryan, William R. "Bank Adjustments to Monetary Policy: Alternative Estimates of the Lag." *American Economic Review,* vol. 57 (September 1967), 855-864.

Cagan, Philip, and Arthur Gandolfi. "The Lag in Monetary Policy as Implied by the Time Pattern of Monetary Effects on Interest Rates." *American Economic Review Papers and Proceedings.* vol. 59 (May 1969), 277-284.

Culbertson, J.M. "Friedman on the Lag in Effect of Monetary Policy." *Journal of Political Economy,* vol. 68 (December 1960), 617-621.

de Leeuw, Frank, and Edward Gramlich. "The Federal Reserve–MIT Econometric Model." *Federal Reserve Bulletin,* vol. 54 (January 1968), 11-40.

Friedman, Milton. "The Lag in Effect of Monetary Policy." *Journal of Political Economy,* vol. 69 (October 1961), 447-466.

________ "A Monetary and Fiscal Framework for Economic Stability." *American Economic Review,* vol. 38 (June 1948), 245-264.

________ "Price, Income, and Monetary Changes in Three Wartime Periods." *American Economic Review,* vol. 42 (May 1952), 612-625.

________ "The Role of Monetary Policy." *American Economic Review,* vol. 58 (March 1968), 1-17.

________ "A Theoretical Framework for Monetary Analysis." *Journal of Political Economy,* vol. 78 (March/April 1970), 193-235.

________ and Gary S. Becker. "A Statistical Illusion in Judging Keynesian Models." *Journal of Political Economy,* vol. 65 (February 1957), 64-75.

________ and Anna J. Schwartz. "Money and Business Cycles." *Review of Economics and Statistics,* vol. 45, no. 1, part 2: Supplement (February 1963), 32-64.

Gibson, William E. "The Lag in Effect of Monetary Policy on Income and Interest Rates." *Quarterly Journal of Economics,* vol. 84 (May 1970), 288-300.

Hay, Keith A.J. "Money and Cycles in Post-Confederation Canada." *Journal of Political Economy,* vol. 75 (June 1967), 263-273.

Macesich, George. "The Rate of Change in Money Stock as a Leading Canadian Indicator." *Canadian Journal of Economics and Political Science,* vol. 28 (August 1962), 424-430.

Mayer, Thomas. "The Inflexibility of Monetary Policy." *Review of Economics and Statistics,* vol. 50 (November 1958), 358-374.

_________ "The Lag in Effect of Monetary Policy: Some Criticisms." *Western Economic Journal,* vol. 7 (September 1965), 324-342.

Rhomberg, R.R. "A Model of the Canadian Economy under Fixed and Flexible Exchange Rates." *Journal of Political Economy,* vol. 72 (February 1964), 1-31.

Simons, Henry C. "Rule Versus Authority in Monetary Policy." *Journal of Political Economy,* vol. 44 (February 1936), 1-30.

Slutsky, Eugen. "The Summation of Random Causes as a Source of Cyclic Processes." *Econometrica,* vol. 5 (April 1937), 105-147.

Smith, Warren L. "A Graphical Exposition of the Complete Keynesian System." *Southern Economic Journal,* vol. 23 (October 1956), 115-125.

Sprinkel, Beryl. "Monetary Growth as a Cyclical Predictor." *Journal of Finance,* vol. 14 (September 1959), 333-346.

Tanner, J. Ernest. "Lags in the Effects of Monetary Policy: A Statistical Investigation." *American Economic Review,* vol. 59 (December 1969), 794-805.

Tobin, James. "The Interest Elasticity of the Transactions Demand for Cash." *Review of Economics and Statistics,* vol. 38 (August 1956), 241-247.

Tucker, Donald P. "Dynamic Income Adjustment to Money Supply Changes." *American Economic Review,* vol. 56 (June 1966), 433-449.

Walters, A.A. "Monetary Multipliers in the United Kingdom 1880-1962." *Oxford Economic Papers,* vol. 18 (November 1966), 270-283.

Warburton, Clark. "Bank Reserves and Business Fluctuations." *Journal of the American Statistical Association,* vol. 43 (December 1948), 547-558.

________ "The Theory of Turning Points in Business Fluctuations." *Quarterly Journal of Economics,* vol. 64 (November 1950), 525-549.

Miscellaneous

Federal Reserve Bulletin. Vol. 50 (February 1964), 154.

Federal Reserve Bulletin. Vol. 53 (July 1967), 1168-1169.

Federal Reserve Bulletin. Vols. 54 and 55 (November 1968 through May 1969).

Federal Reserve Bulletin. Vol. 56 (January 1970), A42.

Letter from William McChesney Martin, Jr. to Dr. Wayne C. Grover published in *Federal Reserve Bulletin,* vol. 50 (August 1964).

Joint Economic Committee, "The Supply of Money and Changes in Prices and Output," by Milton Friedman, *The Relationship of Prices to Economic Stability and Growth.* 85th Cong., 2d Sess. Washington, D.C.: Government Printing Office, 1958.

Author Index

Numbers in brackets are reference numbers and indicate that an author's work is referred to although his name is not cited in the text. Underlined numbers give the page on which the complete reference is listed.

Subject Index